The Observers Series
CANALS

About the Book

Britain's canals – dramatically revived in recent years – offer a fascinating study on foot, on a boat, by car or even in an armchair, but there have been few simple basic books on the subject.

This book condenses a remarkable amount of information, from the canal-digging 'navvies' to the present revival scene. It looks especially at our waterways now – at the intriguing locks, tunnels, aqueducts, bridges, boats and other sights to seek out.

There is a descriptive canal list, maps, a wealth of cruising photographs, and a widely-varied source-list for deeper study.

About the Author

Formerly teacher, trainer of teachers and schools adviser, John Gagg has written many educational books now in wide use both in Britain and overseas. At the same time he has studied and cruised on the whole of our inland canal and river system, taken 20,000 photographs, and written twelve books and hundreds of articles on our canals.

He lectures frequently on inland waterways, and is an active member of the Inland Waterways Association, which has campaigned successfully since 1946 for the use and revival of canals for both commerce and leisure.

The *Observer's* series was launched in 1937 with the publication of *The Observer's Book of Birds*. Today, fifty years later, paperback *Observers* continue to offer practical, useful information on a wide range of subjects, and with every book regularly revised by experts, the facts are right up-to-date. Students, amateur enthusiasts and professional organisations alike will find the latest *Observers* invaluable.

'Thick and glossy, briskly informative' – *The Guardian*

'If you are a serious spotter of any of the things the series deals with, the books must be indispensable' – *The Times Educational Supplement*

OBSERVERS

CANALS

John Gagg

with photographs by the author
and drawings by Robert Wilson

BLOOMSBURY BOOKS
LONDON

PENGUIN BOOKS

Published by the Penguin Group
Penguin Books Ltd, 27 Wrights Lane, London W8 5TZ, England
Penguin Books USA Inc., 375 Hudson Street, New York, New York 10014, USA
Penguin Books Australia Ltd, Ringwood, Victoria, Australia
Penguin Books Canada Ltd, 2801 John Street, Markham, Ontario, Canada L3R 1B4
Penguin Books (NZ) Ltd, 182-190 Wairau Road, Auckland 10, New Zealand

Penguin Books Ltd, Registered Offices: Harmondsworth, Middlesex, England

First published 1982
New edition 1988

This edition published by Bloomsbury Books, an imprint of
Godfrey Cave Associates', 42 Bloomsbury Street, London, WC1B 3QJ,
under licence from Penguin Books Limited, 1992

1 3 5 7 9 10 8 6 4 2

Copyright © John Gagg, 1982, 1988
Originally published as *The Observer's Book of Canals* in small hardback format

All rights reserved

Printed and bound in Great Britain by
BPCC Hazells Ltd

Member of BPCC Ltd

ISBN 1-8547-1023-0

CONTENTS

This book must be dedicated to the many enthusiasts of the nationwide Inland Waterways Association, and of numerous local societies and trusts, without whose efforts over the years many canals would, without doubt, be no longer usable.

FOREWORD

by Sir Frank Price, DL, FSVA, FCIT
Former Chairman, British Waterways Board

This book could have been entitled 'Every Man's Guide to the Waterways'. However, the more simple choice 'Canals' gives a clue to its author – clear, understandable, uncomplicated.

John Gagg loves his subject and it shows. The book is both well illustrated and overflowing with fascinating and useful information gathered *en route* – no armchair author, this one.

It opens up a new world to the uninitiated, and underlines facets along the system that many old stagers may have failed to see. The world of the waterways is truly a moving feast and it is ours to share and to enjoy.

Observers Canals will be a companion, both to those who have yet to be bitten by the canal bug, and to the many thousands of enthusiasts who share the author's infatuation and deep concern for our neglected canal heritage which he, along with others, is helping to preserve.

INTRODUCTION

This book doesn't pretend to be a significant piece of research on canals. Detailed descriptions have been provided by many other books, notably Charles Hadfield's monumental works. What I hope to offer is the basic information about canals which usually requires a considerable search either in many other books on the subject or in a few large volumes such as encyclopedias. Something easily portable that can be taken along canals, on foot or by boat, has long been needed. I hope that this book satisfies that need. It sketches the beginning of the canal story from man's first use of rivers, describes the remarkable work of the early canal engineers and the 'navvies', and looks at the problems they encountered.

It then observes canals as they are today. It looks at the locks and how they are operated, at the massive tunnels and aqueducts, at the boats and boatmen as they were and now are. It describes especially the present wide use of waterways for pleasure, how you can hire a boat, walk a towpath, or go fishing.

There are potted descriptions (with lengths and numbers of locks) of all the waterways now in use or partial use, a glossary and a detailed list of books, maps, guides, museums, etc., for further information.

I hope that this book will prove a handy companion for anyone with an interest in our fascinating waterways – or that it may help to rouse an interest.

John Gagg

1   WHAT IS A CANAL?

There is always some confusion over defining a 'canal'. Strictly speaking it is a waterway dug by man, as distinct from a river. But many rivers, nowadays, contain lengths artificially dug in order to make them more easily navigable. Conversely, some 'canals' incorporate lengths of river in places.

In usage, then, the word 'canal' in Britain is applied loosely to most of the waterway network, spreading out from the pure canals of the Midlands to various river-based navigations around the outskirts. After some miles, of course, all these outer rivers free themselves from locks and artificial cuts and become open (and tidal) to the sea. The Severn becomes tidal at Gloucester. The Nene and the Great Ouse are controlled, with locks, down to Peterborough and Denver respectively. The Yorkshire Ouse is free and tidal for some way inland, almost to York. The Trent is free almost to Newark, the Thames up to Teddington. Yet even some of these tidal river lengths form links between canals.

Although this book is concerned mainly with pure 'canals', it must frequently venture along the rivers which those canals join, or of which they are part, or which link canals. Certainly anyone who cruises on canals for pleasure is very likely to take in a river, or part of a river, on some of his journeys.

Most canals, now, as well as several rivers, are controlled by the British Waterways Board. However

– and happily – they retain their names from the past, unlike the railways. These names derive from the Canal Companies which originally dug the waterways, or from subsequent mergers or takeovers. There is hardly a trace left of our former railway names, but the canals still flaunt theirs despite nationalization. This is one of the delights of looking at them. Although nearly all are linked in a fascinating network, each still has its character, visible in many distinctive ways. It is hoped that this book will bring out much of this delight.

2 WATER AS A MEANS OF TRANSPORT

If you lived across the Channel you would see a great
deal of activity on inland waters, for there you would
find many rivers and canals carrying laden barges. In
Britain, water transport is not a major form of inland
transport. Instead we have vast juggernauts clogging
the roads, annoying people, and damaging roads and
sometimes buildings. And we still have a network of
main railway lines.

A careful search is necessary, however, to find
goods carried on inland waterways. There are still
barges on parts of the Thames, the Lee, the Trent and
the Severn, and on several canals, especially in
Yorkshire. Two canals – the Manchester Ship Canal
and the Gloucester & Sharpness Canal – take sea-
going ships, as does the river Weaver. You can also
find a few smaller canal boats carrying goods on
narrow canals, but these waterways are very shallow
for goods-carrying nowadays, and they are used
mostly by pleasure craft.

Apart from the above examples, we make far too
little use of water transport now compared with other
European countries, and this is a mystery to many
people. In the days before railways, lorries and cars,
transport by water was vital. Land travel then was by
means of horses and wagons or stage-coaches, and
roads were mostly in a bad condition. But where
there were rivers – if they were not too shallow or

fast-flowing – boats were widely used. Not only can a boat carry much more than a horse or even a cart, but little time and money is needed for the upkeep of a river, compared with the cost of building and maintaining a road. So from early times men made primitive boats and used them on the rivers.

There were problems to be overcome. Some regions lacked rivers and elsewhere hilly country made the rivers too swift or too shallow for transport. The idea of digging artificial waterways for the use of boats was put forward and the first canals were created.

There may be a canal – or the remains of a canal – near your home, for at one time many companies were formed to dig them in various parts of the country. Your nearest canal may still be used for carrying goods, but it is more likely to be used for pleasure boats – at least in summer. Many of the original canals fell into disuse, and became largely unnavigable. Two such striking canals – the Huddersfield Narrow and the Rochdale – run over the Pennines between Yorkshire and Lancashire. Parts of the Montgomery Canal have fallen into decay, too, but these and others are rapidly being restored. Thus where you find a derelict canal marked on the OS map, volunteers, backed by official support, may well be helping to restore it at this moment. And at long last the British Waterways Board has even improved a commercial waterway – in South Yorkshire.

3 MAN'S EARLY USE OF RIVERS

Man has travelled on water from time immemorial. He no doubt rode astride logs before learning to hollow them out and paddle them along. He made light (and thus portable) coracles of animal skins, and later more elaborate canoes and rowing boats. Then he learnt to use the wind by means of sails. They were not always helpful along rivers inland for the wind might be in the wrong direction, and a river might be too narrow for a boat to tack from side to side. As a result, men used horses, mules or donkeys to pull boats along some rivers. Great barges which carried goods up the Severn, for example, were even pulled by teams of men.

In fact, getting about by water was a heaven-sent form of transport at one time. It is salutary to think of the problems of travelling and carrying goods on land hundreds of years ago, before there were any lorries, cars, trains or good roads. Tracks for pack-horses or wagons were treacherous or even dangerous, so that navigable rivers were full of a variety of boats, from small rowing-boats to large sailing-boats, from small passenger-boats to heavy barges.

There were different-shaped boats with different names on different rivers. There were Severn **trows**, Norfolk **wherries**, **keels** on the Tyne and Humber, and other types of vessels in other areas. These different shapes and uses are in themselves an interesting study. A glance at a map will show how

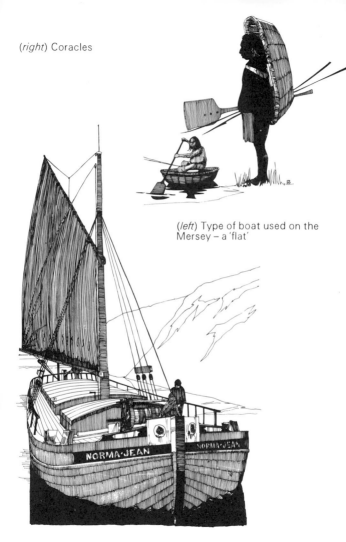

(*right*) Coracles

(*left*) Type of boat used on the Mersey – a 'flat'

NORMA·JEAN

many rivers were available for boats, and thus how useful transport by water could be. This led to the growth of many important towns along the rivers.

Improving the Rivers

During this time in our history, it was still difficult to travel in areas not close to rivers, and some rivers were unsuitable for transport. Around 1600, for example, there were only about 700 miles of navigable rivers — mostly parts of the Severn, Thames, Great Ouse, Nene, Trent and Yorkshire Ouse. There were large areas of the country which were nowhere near a navigable waterway.

This was partly because there were no rivers – or there were only small, swift, shallow ones – in hilly country. But it was also partly because long stretches on even bigger rivers had become impassable for boats. Often rich landowners had built weirs across to catch fish. Bridges and fords prevented boats from passing. Millers blocked rivers with other weirs to divert the water into channels which would drive their mills. River weeds grew thickly in some places.

As trade grew, people wanted to extend navigable lengths of river, and they began to do this in a number of ways. They cut down the weeds and dredged mud away from shallow places. They straightened some of the bends and strengthened banks to prevent them from falling into the river. But the most important improvements were inventions to allow boats through the fish-weirs and mill-weirs which blocked so many waterways. These weirs were of course dams, so getting boats through them was difficult.

Various kinds of openings were made, with names such as **flash-locks**, **staunches**, **water-gates** or **navigation weirs**. Some of these gaps were opened by removing boards with handles, called **slats**, **slackers**, **cloughs** ('clows') or **paddles**. Others had swinging gates which could be dragged open against the force of the flowing river. Staunches were often opened by means of large wooden doors which slid upwards in a framework. There were many of these on rivers in eastern England. All these openings allowed water to pass through, and a boat going downriver could go through with it. Boats travelling upstream had to be dragged through, maybe with winches, against the current.

Pound-locks and Cuts

The millers or fishermen who owned the weirs were not helpful in letting boatmen through for obvious reasons. A lot of water would run through the openings before they could be closed again, and the millers or fishermen then had to wait for the level to build up once more. Moreover, the water that had run through helped boats lower down by ensuring they didn't go aground, but the water above the weir might remain shallow for hours – or even days – in summer. So the boats on that side, as well as the weir-owners, were inconvenienced.

People put up with this for a long time, and there was plenty of argument, but the problem was overcome at last by the use of what are correctly called **pound-locks**; these are the 'locks' which are seen frequently on canals and many rivers. Their great importance was that they allowed boats through

weirs without letting a great deal of water pass through from above the weir. In time, weirs were even built especially to slow rivers down, and to keep the water deep enough for boats where once it had been too shallow. With pound-locks a weir could be a help and not a hindrance.

A pound lock is, in a way, two flash-lock openings close together, and the first ones to be used in England were built near Exeter just before 1567. In 1632 three were built on the Thames to help boats below Oxford – but awkward flash-locks remained along the Thames for a long time after this. Gradually more and more pound-locks were built on rivers as water transport increased.

Another important river improvement was the digging of artificial channels, or 'cuts'. Their purpose might be to straighten winding stretches, or to lead the boats to a pound-lock and back to the main river again. They were important not only because they improved river navigation, but because they showed that men were capable of digging out waterways of their own when necessary. This led, later, to the true canals.

With these various improvements, by the year 1700 boats could navigate on about 1300 miles of rivers and their tributaries. They could reach York, Leeds, Halifax, Burton-on-Trent, Peterborough, Bedford and many other towns situated on rivers. Water transport was an essential part of the life of the country, and men planned developments to many existing waterways, in addition to building new waterways which were not close to any rivers.

4 THE CANAL EXPLOSION

The First Canals

As the use of rivers grew with the building of locks
and weirs, more artificial channels were dug, both to
the mills and to locks, and also to straighten winding
lengths of river. Drainage channels had been dug, too,
in areas such as the Fens, and boats were used on the
bigger ones. Even nowadays the Middle Level Drains,
between the rivers Nene and Great Ouse, are similar
to canals, and boats can cruise for nearly 100 miles on
them.

The ability to dig artificial canals made two
developments possible. Firstly, waterways could be
made where there were no rivers, or to join river to
river. Secondly, with the aid of locks and an assured
water supply, canals could even be constructed in
hilly country.

At this time in our history, factories were being
built and needed supplies of coal. Transport by road
was unsuitable because of the poor roads, so men
looked to the use of boats on inland waterways, and
eventually to more artificial waterways. This speeded
the development of new canals.

The Romans had in fact dug a number of canals in
Britain, including the Fossdyke which still links the
river Trent with the river Witham. The town of
Exeter dug the Exeter Canal for just under two miles
alongside the river Exe in the 16th century, and this
had pound-locks. The French had the Canal de Briare,

In the Middle Level Drains today

36 locks in 35 miles, by 1642, and the Canal du Midi, 149 miles and 100 locks – some quite spectacular – by 1681. Meanwhile, in England, an artificial cut from Stamford by the river Welland, with eight locks, was open by the 1670s.

There was extensive work on rivers, with dredging and the making of locks, as the 17th century ended and the 18th began; the Weaver, the Aire, the Douglas, the Kennet, the Bristol Avon, the Don and others were made navigable, often with artificial cuts. The Yorkshire Derwent was usable up to Malton by 1723 – an ironic thought in view of some opposition nowadays to restoring that river for boats.

As to our first true canal, if you leave out the Fossdyke, and think of the Exeter Canal and the Stamford Canal as cuts to bypass awkward lengths of rivers, the honour of the first British canal belongs to

Bridgewater Canal at Worsley. In the distance is the exit from the underground mines which gave rise to the historic original Bridgewater Canal

Ireland. There, in 1742, the Newry Canal was completed, 18 miles long with 14 locks, running from the river Bann to Newry. The impressive Grand Canal, in Ireland too, was begun in 1756, but this struggled for very many years before completion.

In England, a pupil of the Newry Canal's engineer produced, in 1757, an artificial canal in the guise of a river improvement. Ostensibly making the Sankey Brook navigable from St Helens to the Mersey, it was in fact entirely a lateral canal fed by the river. This waterway (like the Newry Canal) is often forgotten when anyone talks of the 'first British canal'. This label is usually given to the Bridgewater Canal, presumably because it was the first canal in **England** independent of a river. Certainly it gets all the publicity and the credit for the start of the craze for canal digging.

It was built for the Duke of Bridgewater to take coal from his mines at Worsley to Manchester. Much of it was finished by 1761 and it is still used today. It even had branches underground into the coal-mines, and it crossed the river Irwell on a bridge of its own, which people thought wonderful. The canal was later lengthened, and it certainly began the busy years of goods-carrying and canal-digging which seemed to send Britain somewhat hysterical.

Canal Mania

All over the country men had ideas for digging canals – from their towns to others, or to mines, factories or rivers. They formed companies to finance their projects, but they had first to obtain the approval of Parliament for each canal proposed. Some people objected to a canal running through their property and there were often long arguments and delays. Canal after canal was authorized, though some were never dug, and other ventures ran out of money again and again.

Some proposed canals were very short, but one of the first to be mooted was the lengthy Grand Trunk, now called the Trent & Mersey. This not only served the factories in the pottery towns of Staffordshire, but it also – as its present name indicates – joined the river Trent with the river Mersey, running from one side of England to the other.

There are several names in the gallery of canal engineers, but perhaps James Brindley's is best known. There were of course no trained canal engineers, and Brindley's original job was as a millwright. He had to learn about canal planning and construction by

Present-day scene in the Potteries where one of the first big canals – now called the Trent & Mersey – originated

actually doing it. He planned, built, or helped with the making of many canals in his lifetime, as well as training engineers who built other canals. He also advocated the wide use of canals, and travelled thousands of miles on horseback to meetings and to see how digging was getting on.

The 'Navigators'

So the canals were dug – and digging it was! All the tools available in those days were picks and shovels and wheelbarrows.

Large gangs of labourers moved about the country. They were rough and noisy, and often frightened people living in quiet villages. Because they were building waterways for boats to navigate, these men came to be called **navigators**, hence the present-day word **navvy**. It seems unbelievable that every bit of earth to make the canal channels was moved by navvies' shovels. They dug out the locks, too, with more skilled colleagues building the chambers. Where the ground was not level they piled up embankments or dug out cuttings – for, of course, the canal had to be level in between locks or the water would run away. In the early days, though, the canal routes tended to meander and follow the contours to avoid moving too much earth.

The most remarkable work of the canal builders was the digging of tunnels. These tunnels usually occurred after a canal had climbed fairly high up a hillside; hills were a special problem for the engineers.

The hillier the country, the more essential it was to make sure that there was a good water-supply. Every time a lock is used it runs away a lot of water from higher up, and this water has to come from some reliable source. Some canals took their water from rivers, but on higher ground the engineers had to find other ways of obtaining water. It was necessary, of

Tools used to dig canals

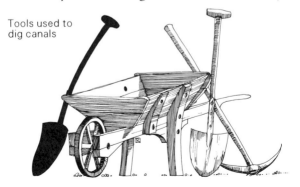

24

course, to have a water-supply to the highest level (called the **summit level**) to allow for the water passing through the locks. The engineers usually planned a reservoir near this summit level to keep it supplied with water. Sometimes water was pumped up to the summit from a reservoir lower down, as on the Kennet & Avon Canal. Water for the high canals near Birmingham was also pumped from deep shafts below ground.

The engineers had to decide how high they could take a canal before it would become too difficult to keep the summit filled with water. They also had to consider the expense of digging locks as the canal kept on climbing. The locks were not only expensive to build, but they used up water and slowed down boats. Thus there would come a time when a builder would decide not to climb any higher, but to dig a tunnel through the hill instead. There was also the task of building many bridges and some aqueducts.

The efforts of the navvies were back-breaking. Several canals were dug over the Pennines, needing many locks to climb up and then down again. The Leeds & Liverpool Canal is still in use there, and active Societies exist which are eager to restore the other Pennine crossings. Another great link was the Kennet & Avon Canal between the Thames and the Severn. Parts of this canal were unhappily allowed to go out of use, but it is now almost entirely restored.

The Forth was linked with the Clyde in Scotland and the Severn linked through the busy industrial Midlands to the Trent & Mersey. The Trent & Mersey was also joined to the Thames at Oxford, by means of the Coventry Canal and the Oxford Canal.

25

An unusual bridge in one of the many cuttings on the Shropshire Union Canal. Cuttings and embankments helped to make the canal take a straighter course

With their shovels and barrows, and perhaps horses, the navigators dug canals all over the country. They climbed hills by means of great flights of locks and burrowed through the higher hills. The canals dug in the earlier days seemed to wander for miles round low hills in order to remain on level ground and not have locks. But later engineers such as Thomas Telford planned straighter canals, using the soil from cuttings to make huge embankments across valleys.

Water did not soak through the canal beds because **puddle** had been used in most places. This was a mixture of the right kind of earth and water spread up to three feet thick to line the bed underneath a layer of ordinary soil. Often clay and water were made into puddle by men treading it down for hour after hour.

As the navvies dug and puddled and moved along the route, other men worked to make bricks or cut stone, for building bridges, locks and aqueducts, or for lining the tunnels. Boatbuilders, also, were busy constructing boats both for the canal engineers to use as the water was let in, and for the goods carriers who quickly followed.

Rivers and canals were linked so that boats could move from one canal to another. People realized that if locks were of different sizes on different canals this would be a hindrance, so some of the canal companies met in conference to discuss this. Eventually, two main sizes of lock appeared, which are described on p. 59, the 'narrow' canal locks which could contain a boat 7 ft (2.13 m) wide and about 70 ft (21.34 m) long, and the 'broad' locks which were twice as wide or more.

These latter took **barges** of 14 ft (4.27 m) in width, or instead a side-by-side pair of **narrow boats** from the narrow-lock canals. Some of the 'broad' canals – such as the Leeds & Liverpool – have locks shorter than 70 ft. There are still other exceptions to the two main lock-sizes, but boats about 7 ft wide can go almost everywhere, if they are not longer than about 57 ft (17.68 m).

It was unfortunate that this 7 ft width was ever decided on, for it means that most of our canals are unable to take large boats, while in other countries the locks are usually much bigger, and huge barges are able to carry vast quantities of goods cheaply and efficiently. In Britain, nothing was ever done to increase the size of our narrow locks, so it does not pay to carry most goods on the narrow canals any longer. But if canals are ever enlarged, or new ones built, there is no reason why we should not be as up to date with water transport as other countries.

In the days of the canal mania boats were soon travelling between many different places, and all over the country there was transport by thousands of boats pulled by horses or mules; the boats carried passengers as well as goods.

It may be difficult for us to imagine the vast amount of digging, tunnelling, bridge-building and lock-making, and the resultant boats travelling everywhere. But we can look at the noisy and damaging traffic on our roads nowadays, and at least think how much quieter and more peaceful the horses and boats on the waterways must have been.

In the days of the canal mania in Britain, these new artificial cuts, and the rivers which they joined, were for many years our main transport highways. The map on p. 30 shows rivers and canals in use by about 1850.

Opening a Canal

Whenever a new canal was completed and ready to start carrying boats, there was often a great ceremony. Bands would play, processions marched, and there would be a string of boats carrying the important people of the district. Amid the flags and other decorations, there would probably be a lavish dinner

'Narrow boats' – whether for commerce or pleasure – are built to fit the 'narrow locks' found on most of the Midland canals

with much wine. Elsewhere, the men who had actually dug the canal would have barrels of beer and maybe share a roast ox, while guns fired. It was a great occasion for all the towns and villages along the length of the new waterway.

Rivers and canals in use around 1850

The following are the approximate dates when the main canals which are still in use were first opened. In some cases parts had still to be completed, and many branches were added.

Fossdyke – about AD 120

Bridgewater – part 1761, main 1765

Staffordshire & Worcestershire – 1772

Ripon – 1772

Birmingham (main line) – 1772

Sir John Ramsden's (Huddersfield Broad) – 1776

Chesterfield – 1777

Trent & Mersey – 1777

Caldon – about 1779

Stourbridge – 1779

Erewash 1779

Chester (now part of Shropshire Union) – 1779

Birmingham & Fazeley – 1789

Oxford 1790

Coventry – 1790

Wirral (now part of Shropshire Union) – 1795

Ashton – 1796

Warwick & Birmingham, and Warwick & Napton (now part of Grand Union) – 1800

Peak Forest – 1800

Stainforth & Keadby – 1802

Leek (branch of Caldon) – 1802

Ashby – 1804

Grand Junction (now part of Grand Union) – 1805

Llangollen (to Pontcysyllte) – 1805; to Llangollen – 1808

Crinan (Scotland) – 1809

Kennet & Avon – 1810

Brecon & Abergavenny – 1812

Grand Union Leicester line (present name) – 1814. (Parts in 1778, 1794, 1797, 1809)

Worcester & Birmingham 1815

Leeds & Liverpool – 1816 (Rufford Branch 1781)

Stratford-upon-Avon – 1816

Pocklington – 1818

Lancaster – 1819

Caledonian (Scotland) 1822

Gloucester & Sharpness – 1827

Macclesfield – 1831

Middlewich (now part of Shropshire Union) – 1833

Birmingham & Liverpool Junction (now main part of Shropshire Union) – 1835

Manchester Ship Canal – 1894

New Junction – 1905

5 TUNNELS, AQUEDUCTS AND BRIDGES

The easiest canals to dig were those that merely ran across flat country from one place to another. They needed few if any locks, though of course they required many bridges where they cut through farms, across roads, or even across footpaths. In hillier country the engineering problems were greater. More locks were necessary, water-supply could be difficult, tunnels might be needed, and where rivers were crossed aqueducts had to be built.

Tunnels

The most difficult job of all was boring the tunnels. These might have to be through small hills which lay in the path of the canal, or more likely they were needed after the canal had already climbed for some distance by means of locks towards the higher land.

Tunnel-making was no easy job in the days before machinery. A huge hole had to be made through the ground. This had to be level, so that when the water was let in it wouldn't just run out again; and the tunnel had to be straight. The canal builders, quite apart from having no machines, knew very little about this kind of work. The only people who could help them were those concerned with coalmines, for they were used to tunnelling underground. As it happened, the Bridgewater Canal itself connected

with many small tunnels into the Duke's mines at
Worsley

Very often work started on different parts of a
canal tunnel at the same time. Shafts were dug straight
down from the top of the hill to the level where the
tunnel was to be. Men were then lowered down the
shafts and started digging sideways to make the
tunnel. The soil and rock were lifted up the shafts to
the hilltop in the same large buckets that the men
travelled down in. Some tunnels still have ventilation
'chimneys' above these shafts.

It must have been unpleasant underground, for the
work was done by candlelight, and the men had to
use gunpowder if they needed to remove rock. The
air might be foul, water might come flooding in from

underground springs and, of course, the roof could fall in. Many navvies were killed and injured doing this work, and the scene underground must have been eerie in the light of the candles and of the fires which would be lit under the shafts. These helped to ventilate the underground workings by sending hot air up the shafts and thus drawing in fresh air in its place.

Tunnel builders never knew for certain what sort of ground they would be digging in. It might be solid rock or it might be soft wet sand. This latter was especially difficult, and sometimes the line of a tunnel had to be changed entirely to avoid it. Many tunnels took much longer to build than the planners expected. Blisworth tunnel on the present Grand Union Canal had to be built in a different direction because of water flooding in, and it was not opened until five years after the rest of the canal. During that time goods were unloaded at one end and taken over the hill to be put into other boats at the other end.

As the tunnels were dug out they had to be lined with brick or stone unless the rock was very solid. It was amazing how straight some of the long tunnels were after being dug in this way, though there are slight noticeable kinks in a number of them.

The first big tunnel was Brindley's at Harecastle on the Trent & Mersey. It is now closed because over the years it sank, but it was a wonderful achievement when it was dug. Many people didn't believe that its construction was possible; Brindley himself died before it was finished. Water had to be constantly pumped out by pumps driven by wind and water, or by early steam engines, and it was eleven years before this $1\frac{1}{2}$-mile long hole through the hill was open to

The remarkable Harecastle Tunnel near Stoke-on-Trent. The first – now subsided – tunnel can be seen on the left. The present tunnel has needed costly repairs, but provides a vital section of the canal system

boats, in 1777.

As it was not wide enough for boats to pass each other, a new tunnel was dug alongside in 1827. Engineers had learnt much in the meantime, so this tunnel took only two years to build. It is 2,668 m (2919 yd) long and is still in use today although it, too, has sunk in places, and boats use it with great care.

Taking a boat through a canal tunnel is a strange and sometimes alarming experience, although boats must carry headlamps. When you enter some of the longest tunnels you may not even be able to see the far end if the day is misty. The walls are often wet and slimy, and perhaps small stalactites hang from the roof. There may be a few large ventilation shafts up above giving occasional quick glimpses of the sky. Sometimes torrents of water fall down these from

Practising 'legging' through a tunnel

springs, so it is a good idea for the boat steerer to wear a raincoat or use an umbrella.

Most – though not all – tunnels are wide enough for boats to pass, but even then passing is a tight squeeze. You see a headlamp coming for some time before you reach each other, but when you pass you can see very little of the other boat. As you creep by you may collect some of the dirt from the walls, or even some soot – still there from the days of steam engines. And of course you may meet the ghost of Kit Crewbucket, said to haunt several tunnels!

Kit's origins are a mystery. Sometimes called Kit Crew, some think he (she?) comes from 'Kidsgrove Boggart' – a boggart, or bogeyman, from Kidsgrove north of Harecastle tunnel. How did Kit get to Crick tunnel, then, in Northamptonshire, or indeed to several other tunnels?

Nowadays boats are driven through tunnels by

their engines, but before these were invented men had to use their legs, for few tunnels had towpaths for the horses. While the horses were taken over the top, **leggers** perhaps went to help the boatmen. They lay out from the side of the boat and 'legged' it through by walking on the tunnel sides or roof. They were paid very little, though it must have been extremely hard work. At one time the leggers at Harecastle took three hours to get a boat through and were given 7½p each for the work.

Even after the invention of steam engines, their use was forbidden in some tunnels because of the problems of ventilation. Sometimes tugs pulled trains of boats through. One at the new Harecastle tunnel was driven by electricity and had to pull a boat carrying 18 tons of batteries. At some of the other Trent & Mersey tunnels tugs had wheels at their sides to run along the tunnel walls. A few tunnels had handrails so that boatmen could pull their boats through.

The longest canal tunnel in Britain is at Standedge in the Pennines, 5208 m (3 miles 418 yd) long on the Huddersfield Narrow Canal. This canal is not usable at the moment, but inspection boats still go into the tunnel. Much of it is rock, with no brick lining, and it is narrow and low. There are special passing-places for boats. When the tunnel was completed in 1811, 500 people went through in boats with a band playing, while 10,000 others came to watch. The first boats took an hour and forty minutes to pass through.

The longest tunnel recently in use is the 2884 m (3154 yd) Dudley tunnel near Birmingham, but this is very low and many boats are too high to pass. It is really three separate tunnels — one long and two short – with gaps between them open to the sky. The longest part is closed at the moment, but a trip boat uses part of the rest. It is near the Black Country Museum.

The longest tunnel used by all kinds of canal boats is the one at Blisworth near the Waterways Museum at Stoke Bruerne. This is 2794 m (3056 yd) long. The last big tunnel to be dug in Britain is also a very long one at Netherton, quite near to Dudley. It was dug to relieve Dudley tunnel, and at 2767 m (3027 yd) long is the widest of all the canal tunnels, with a towpath at each side.

The shortest official tunnel is shorter than some of the new motorway bridges. It is Dunsley, on the Staffs & Worcs Canal, and is only 23 m (25 yd) long, and has a towpath.

The last tunnels of all to be constructed were a pair close to each other near Birmingham. They were made in 1974 where a new road had to cross two lines of canal which were in deep cuttings.

There is a story of a cow which fell into the Leeds & Liverpool Canal near Foulridge tunnel, and swam the 1500 m (1640 yd) to the other end, where it was given a bottle of brandy. Besides the ghost of Kit Crewbucket in several tunnels, at Saddington on the Leicester Grand Union there is supposed to be the ghost of a woman without a head!

Some earlier tunnels were opened out, and there is a length of the Oxford Canal which is still called 'The Tunnel', although no tunnel remains. The short Armitage tunnel on the Trent & Mersey – thought to be the first completed on our canals – was opened out in 1971 and is now just a gloomy red rock cutting.

(above) The closed western end of Standedge Tunnel
today – 3 miles 418 yards long

(below) Towpath through Cookley Tunnel on the Staffs
& Worcs Canal

The following are the longest tunnels fully in use:

	metres	yards
Blisworth *Grand Union*	2794	3056
Netherton *Birmingham Canal Navigations*	2768	3027
Harecastle (new) *Trent & Mersey*	2669	2919
West Hill (or Wast Hill) *Worcester &* *Birmingham*	2493	2726
Braunston *Grand Union*	1867	2042
Foulridge *Leeds & Liverpool*	1500	1640
Crick *Grand Union (Leicester Line)*	1397	1528
Preston Brook *Trent & Mersey*	1133	1239
Husbands Bosworth *Grand Union (Leicester Line)*	1066	1166
Islington *Grand Union (Regents Canal)*	878	960
Saddington *Grand Union (Leicester Line)*	805	880
Shortwood *Worcester & Birmingham*	561	613
Tardebigge *Worcester & Birmingham*	530	580
Barnton *Trent & Mersey*	523	572
Gannow *Leeds & Liverpool*	511	559
Gosty Hill *Birmingham Canal Navigations*	509	557

There are 46 tunnels still in use, though on account of their age a few are normally closed for repairs.

Aqueducts

Often the route of a canal ran across streams or rivers. This usually meant crossing on an aqueduct, though sometimes, as at Alrewas on the Trent & Mersey, and at two places on the Oxford Canal, the canal runs into a river and out again. A few canals cross over roads, and in later years railways were sometimes built under canals. Occasionally, canals have to cross over other canals. These water-bridges had to hold the water without leaking, and the early ones were strong

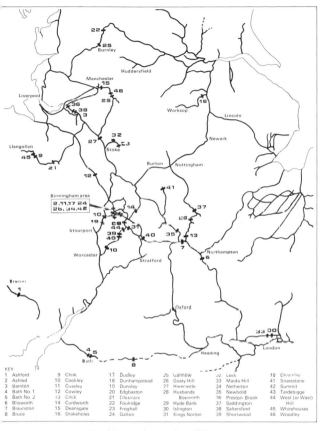

The 46 canal tunnels still in use

stone or brick structures filled with earth or puddle
to make the channel. Later, metal troughs to hold the
water were carried across valleys.

(*above*) The mighty Pontcysyllte Aqueduct in North Wales

(*below*) Crossing the aqueduct, 1007 ft long, and 121 ft above the river Dee at one point

Brindley's Barton aqueduct, made to carry the Bridgewater across the Irwell, was mentioned earlier. Many people didn't believe it was feasible, and when it was completed they came for miles to see boats passing over other boats. Brindley also designed other aqueducts which have become well known. One carries the Trent & Mersey over the river Dove near Burton on 23 arches. Most of these arches are needed to carry the canal over the low ground near the river.

From a boat on the canal it isn't easy to know how often small aqueducts are crossed, but the larger ones can usually be detected because the waterway grows narrower. The most famous aqueduct, Pontcysyllte in North Wales, is only just wide enough for the ordinary 7 ft width of a canal narrow boat. If there is a strong cross-wind, boats cannot help scraping the sides of the metal trough as they cross.

This aqueduct is an incredible sight, especially from the Dee valley below. It is a box-like trough carried on 18 stone pillars. It is 307 m (1007 ft) long, and the water in the river is 37 m (121 ft) below it at one point. There are 418 iron plates making up the trough, and along one side is a towpath and railings. There is nothing at all on the other side except the edge of the trough, so when you look down from a boat you look straight to the ground beneath.

There are some very fine stone aqueducts such as the Dundas aqueduct on the Kennet & Avon near Bath, and another at Avoncliffe on the same canal. A magnificent one carries the Lancaster Canal over the river Lune. It has five great arches, and the canal level is 19 m (62 ft) above the river level. The aqueduct is 183 m (600 ft) long and built of hard sandstone. In

(*above*) The massive Lune aqueduct carrying the Lancaster Canal over the river

(*below*) The Avon aqueduct on the Edinburgh & Glasgow Union Canal

The canal 'flyover' aqueduct at Hazelhurst on the Caldon
Canal

Scotland there are three large aqueducts on the Union
Canal (which is 'closed' but under restoration). The
Avon aqueduct there is 250 m (810 ft) long, on 12
arches, up to 26 m (86 ft) high.

A Grand Union aqueduct over the river Ouse near
Wolverton once collapsed into the river, and some
old locks had to be brought back into use until a new
iron trough was built. Another metal-trough aqueduct is on the Stratford Canal near Bearley. It takes
the waterway over a road and railways, and the
towpath is below water-level.

Some intriguing aqueducts carry canals over other
canals. One is near Birmingham, where the New Line
of the Birmingham to Wolverhampton route was
taken under the original Old Line. (There are two
other canal-over-canal aqueducts on this Old Line).

The Barton Aqueduct, full of water, swinging open over the Manchester Ship Canal

Another carries the Caldon Canal under its own branch to Leek in Staffordshire. A third carries the link from the Trent & Mersey to the Macclesfield Canal over the main line of the Trent & Mersey near Kidsgrove. These might be called 'canal flyovers'.

The most interesting aqueduct of all is the one that now takes the Bridgewater Canal over the Manchester Ship Canal. It replaced the famous Barton aqueduct mentioned earlier. When the Ship Canal was built it was decided to take the Bridgewater over it in a swinging aqueduct. So whenever a ship comes along the canal below, gates are closed across the Bridge-water Canal aqueduct and also across the ends of the canal on land, and the whole aqueduct swings open, full of water, to allow the ships to pass. The tank of this aqueduct is 5.5 m (18 ft) wide, 1.8 m (6 ft) deep and 71.6 m (235 ft) long. Full of water, it weighs

One of the simplest country bridges, with no towpath
under it, on the Trent & Mersey Canal

1400 tons, and it is balanced on one large pier in the
Ship Canal. The old towpath is high above the water.

Here are some other aqueducts still in use and not
mentioned above: Marple on the Peak Forest Canal
(over the river Goyt), Stanley Ferry on the Aire &
Calder (over the river Calder), Stretton on the
Shropshire Union (over the A5 road), Dane on the
Macclesfield (over the river Dane), Tame on the
Coventry (over the river Tame), Priest Holme on the
Leeds & Liverpool (over the river Aire), North
Circular on the Grand Union (over the North
Circular Road in London).

Fixed Bridges

There are many bridges over canals, carrying roads
and, occasionally, footpaths. Some are small hump-
backed bridges built for farm equipment and animals.

A typical farm bridge. This one is on the Monmouthshire & Brecon Canal

A number of these are no longer used.

On most canals the bridges bear small number-plates; people cruising on the canals often need these numbers to show them, from a guide-book, exactly where they are.

Many old bridges have pleasant shapes which vary from canal to canal as do so many other things. Often they are of brick, which may be weathered and worn by now. On canals near hills, such as the Macclesfield and the Leeds & Liverpool, there are great stone bridges. Usually the towpath goes under the bridge, but in a few places the bridges may be only just wide enough for the waterway. The horses would have to be unfastened and taken round unless – as on parts of the Trent & Mersey and the Stratford Canals, for example – there is a slit for the towrope to pass through.

A farm bridge with a tow-rope slit, to save the cost of a towpath underneath. There are several of these on the Stratford Canal

Along the Staffs & Worcs Canal there are attractive nameplates on many bridges, with names such as Giggetty, Wombourn, Bumblehole, Dimmingsdale and Bratch. There are also names on some bridges in the Birmingham Canal Navigations.

Very many bridges are wide enough for only one boat to pass through, and when they are on a bend it can be awkward if boats from both ways arrive at the same time. There are also more recent larger bridges where roads have been widened. Where motorways cross canals, the huge concrete bridges look more like tunnels from the canal.

Lift-up Bridges

The most interesting bridges are those which have to be moved to allow boats through. These are lower than ordinary ones and would have been cheaper to

(*above*) Type of lift-bridge found on the Llangollen Canal

(*below*) Unusual lift-bridge on the Huddersfield Broad Canal. When a handle is turned, the roadway lifts bodily

A lift-bridge on the Oxford Canal, one of many

build. Some of them tip up and some swing round sideways. Those that tip up are called **lift-bridges** or **drawbridges**.

To open such a bridge for a boat it is necessary to pull down the balancing arms. The bridge then lifts up at an angle, but someone may have to sit on the arm or fix it in some way to prevent the bridge from dropping down again. There are many bridges along the Oxford Canal with low balancing arms. On the Llangollen Canal the lift-bridges have high, Dutch-like beams. There are also drawbridges on the Caldon Canal and on the Monmouthshire & Brecon.

You will find a few others elsewhere, including some on the northern Stratford Canal which are wound up with the windlass normally used to operate locks. Others down the Northampton Arm of the

Grand Union usually remain up except when farmers require them. There are a few bigger bridges where the whole roadway rises level instead of tilting. There is one on the river Witham at Lincoln and another on the short Huddersfield Broad Canal.

On the commercial canals in Yorkshire, at Plank Lane near Leigh, and at Gloucester, there are new lift-bridges worked by electricity. There is a small one of these on the Monmouthshire & Brecon at Talybont, and one on the Oxford Canal.

Swing-bridges

The bridges which swing sideways out of the way are not so risky for boats, but sometimes they are difficult to move because of dirt in the mechanism. There are many of these on the Leeds & Liverpool, where someone must push on a long arm to swing the bridge. There are others in a number of places, but perhaps the most interesting ones are on the larger canals and rivers used by barges and in some cases ships.

On the Gloucester & Sharpness Ship Canal all the bridges are movable. A new one at Gloucester lifts up, but all the others swing. Bridge-keepers, living in fascinating little houses, come out and wind a handle, moving round with the bridge as it opens. The ships on this canal can only just squeeze through. There is of course the canal swing-aqueduct at Barton over the Manchester Ship Canal, and there are other road and rail swing-bridges on that canal and elsewhere where ships travel, such as along the river Weaver and the Caledonian Canal.

(*above*) One of over 50 swing-bridges on the Leeds &
Liverpool

(*below*) Swing-bridge on the Birmingham & Fazeley. The
tower has steps up to the footbridge

(*above*) The Gloucester & Sharpness Ship Canal has 15 swing-bridges like this one, opened by hand, and one electric lift-bridge. The coasters just fit the opening

(*below*) Towpath bridge at Bordesley Junction, in Birmingham

On the Aire & Calder Navigation and other commercial waterways there are swing-bridges for the barges and pleasure boats which use these canals. Some work by electricity, but others are opened by hand, sometimes by a bridge-keeper walking round pushing a revolving arm. There is a railway bridge on the Stainforth & Keadby Canal which has to be slid out of the way for boats.

Towpath Bridges

Often the towpath of a canal has to rise over a branch of the canal, or over the junction with another canal. There are some delightful bridges built for this purpose, especially in the Black Country, where there were so many branches and junctions. The cast-iron bridges there are striking; similar ones exist on the north Oxford Canal where former loops were straightened.

Some junction bridges are simple brick or stone ones, as at Great Haywood, Marple and Kingswood. All, of course, needed a gentle slope for the sake of the horse, and often 'ribs' were built in the slope to give a grip.

Turnover Bridges

A particular type of towpath bridge to look for is that used where the path changes sides. Some rather graceful bridges – called **turnover**, **roving** or **changeline** – were built to allow for this, such as one at Foden Bank, near Macclesfield. The aim was to allow the horse to walk up a slope, cross over, and come back facing the boat before turning under the

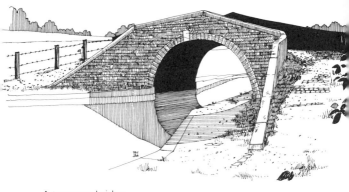

A turnover bridge

same bridge but on the other side of the canal. In this way the rope need not be unfastened.

6 'WORKING A LOCK'

The most important things on canals – the devices that made most canals possible – are the locks. Let us look at these useful inventions.

Locks were first used on rivers to allow boats through weirs without having to let a large amount of water through at the same time. Most of these early weirs were built by millers and fishermen for their own purposes, but men also started to build them to deepen the water-channel for boats, by raising the water-level behind them. Since a weir is a kind of dam, the deeper water allowed larger boats to travel and rivers could be made navigable for greater distances. The weirs (with their locks alongside) were like 'steps' in the river, turning it perhaps from a swift shallow one to a slower one with deep stretches between weirs. This same idea of 'water-steps' was used for making canals, enabling them to climb up slopes.

'Steps' in Waterways

Canals (with the occasional exception) don't flow as rivers do and must remain on the level, but they were often built as a means of taking boats up and down quite steep slopes. Thus the engineers dug level stretches of water, with steps in the form of locks between one level and the next. The stretches between locks are usually called 'pounds', which is confusing when you think of the old name 'pound-lock'. In fact, everyone refers to these as 'locks' nowadays, with canal 'pounds' between them.

The diagram shows roughly what happens at a lock. Between the upper and lower pounds of the canal is a kind of water-box with doors which shut off the ends. The principle is simple, but the actual operation is rather more complicated. If a boat approaches on the higher pound, for example, the water in the lock has to be brought up to the same level. This is done by running water into the lock from up above it. Then the doors, which are usually called 'gates', can be opened so that the boat goes into the lock. The gates are closed after it and the water-openings – usually called **paddles** – are also closed.

Next, water is let out of the lock through paddles at the other end, so that the boat sinks downwards. When it has reached the same level as the water in the lower pound, the bottom gates can be opened and the boat may leave. The gates and paddles are then closed for safety. The reverse operation takes place if a boat wants to go from a lower pound to a higher.

What happens at a lock

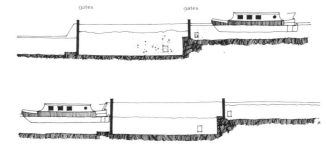

Leaving a narrow lock

This is the working of a lock in theory, but let us look at it in practice. Boats can be seen going through locks every day nowadays, and thousands of people enjoy doing this when they are on holiday in pleasure boats.

Types of Locks

Although all locks operate roughly in the same way, there is a great deal of intriguing variety to be found along canals. A very common kind of lock is on the narrow canals, mostly in the Midlands. These locks, as we saw earlier, are about 7 ft wide by 70 ft long

Two 'narrow boats' side-by-side in a 'broad' lock on the Grand Union Canal

(2.13 m by 21.34 m), and this means that the boats on the canal cannot be bigger than this. These narrow locks usually have two gates at the end next to the lower pound (the 'bottom end'), meeting in the middle and pointing towards the water in the lock. They usually have a single gate at the 'top end', which closes against a solid piece of concrete or stone on the floor of the lock, to hold the gate against the pressure

A river Nene
lock, one of
over 30 with
bottom-end
'guillotine'
gates

of the water. This is the **sill** or **cill**. Sometimes there
is a single gate at the bottom end instead of a pair.

The wider locks on the broad canals are about the
same length as the narrow locks, but roughly twice as
wide. Thus they can hold either a barge 14 ft (4.27 m)
wide or two narrow boats side by side. They have a
pair of gates at each end, which are heavier than the
smaller gates of the narrow canals. There is a broad
lock of this kind alongside the Waterways Museum
at Stoke Bruerne, and many others along the same
canal and elsewhere.

A lock at Fort Augustus on the Caledonian Canal. This will take boats up to 150 ft long and 35 ft wide

An unusual kind of lock-gate can be found on the river Nene. At the bottom end of the river's locks there is a **guillotine gate**. This is made of steel and slides up and down in a large frame. There are two ordinary swinging gates at the other ends of Nene locks. Similar guillotines may be found on other rivers in eastern England, but very few on canals. A lock on the Trent & Mersey has a guillotine gate at each end, and there is a guillotine near Halifax on the Calder & Hebble Navigation.

On most of the commercial canals, and especially on rivers such as the Trent, Weaver and Severn, the locks are bigger than those mentioned above. The Weaver locks will hold quite large ships and so do those on the Manchester Ship Canal and the Caledonian Canal.

The sides of locks are usually built of stone, brick or (more recently) concrete. A few still have wooden parts in their side-walls, and some on the Kennet & Avon Canal, for example, had sloping grassy sides instead of vertical walls, but these are gradually being replaced. A few locks – eg on the Oxford Canal and the Warwickshire Avon – are not oblong in shape, but more like a diamond. There have been round locks in the past, and some still exist in other countries.

The interesting thing about our waterways is that although all locks are just large boxes of water, with some way of getting boats in and out of them, they do differ from each other in various ways all over the country. This is because of the differing ideas of the original companies and engineers. It is intriguing to examine locks to see how much they differ in shape, gates, paddle-gear and other items of lock-furniture. Many of the differences can be seen in photographs reproduced in this book.

Paddle-gear

When the crew of a boat take it through a lock, this is called 'working the lock'. The most important things they have to deal with are the gadgets which let water in and out to change the water-level inside This is done by means of **paddles** uncovering openings under water, and the cogs, rods and so on which work the paddles are generally called **paddle-gear**. **Paddle**, you may recall, was one name given to the boards which were pulled out of the way at the old flash-locks. In some places the name **sluice** is used, and in the north of England the word **clough** (pronounced 'clow') is still widely found. Whatever

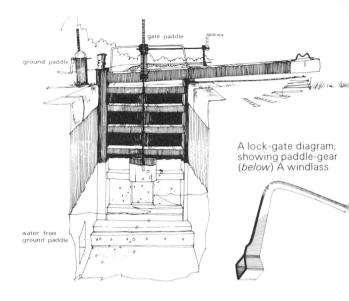

A lock-gate diagram, showing paddle-gear (*below*) A windlass

gate paddle

ground paddle

water from ground paddle

name is used, the apparatus does a simple job. It produces an opening to let water flow through and shuts it again to stop the flow.

In the diagram you can see two different places where paddles let water through. Some slide up and uncover holes in the gates, and some uncover channels under the ground. The first kind is known as a **gate paddle** and the second kind a **ground paddle**. On the Leeds & Liverpool Canal there are paddles which move sideways to uncover holes, instead of moving up and down. There is no need for paddles where there are guillotine gates since the water runs through as soon as the gate begins to rise.

Most paddles are opened and closed by means of an essential tool called a **windlass** (or **key**), shown here.

Incidentally, windlasses are shown as dotted shapes on the paddle-gear in the previous diagram, but they should never be left on their spindles, as they may fly off.

The windlass is placed on the spindle and turned to move cog-wheels which 'open the paddle'. This usually means that they pull up a **rack** at the top of a long rod fastened to the paddle hidden beneath the water. You can see the racks in the diagram of paddle-gear. Winding up a paddle to let water through is sometimes called 'drawing a paddle'. As soon as this is done, water runs through the opening from the higher water-level to the lower one, until both sides are at the same level, then of course it stops. The more paddles there are (or the larger the openings), the more quickly this happens.

There are many different versions of paddle-gear. Some – perhaps unhappily – are being replaced by a standardized and characterless new hydraulic type. A selection of paddle-gear can be seen in the photographs. Obviously the only visible parts are the machinery above the water.

There are several stupid and even dangerous things that people can do when working a lock. If the paddles at both ends are open at the same time, for example, the lock would never 'make a level'. Worse still, a length of canal higher up may be drained. It is also risky ever to let go of a windlass on its spindle. There are many kinds of safety-catches, which you can see in several photographs, aimed at securing the paddle-gear when open, but these should not be trusted. The windlass, if left, could fly round and injure someone, or be lost in the canal.

Different
types of
paddle-gear

Again, if a boat is in a lock and water is being let in, someone must make sure that the boat is held safely, or the force of the water may swing it about and damage it. But, if 'going down', it should not be tied up, or it will 'hang up'. When locking down also, the boat shouldn't be left too far back in the lock, or its stern may settle on the sill which holds back the gates.

Balance-beam

During the process of working a lock, gates have to be opened and closed. As can be seen in many photographs, there is usually a long wooden or metal arm from the gate extending over the land; this is for pushing. It partly balances the weight of the gate also, and is called a **balance-beam**. There is no need to struggle with it, for in any case it is impossible to open a gate before the water-levels are equal. You can just lean your back against it and walk slowly backwards when the gate is ready. It is no use trying to hurry, either. And, simple as this operation sounds, it is highly dangerous for anyone to stand on the lock side of a balance-beam as a gate is opening, or they will be brushed into the lock.

The variety of gear, gates and balance-beams at locks helps to make canals so interesting. There is even gear which needs a handspike instead of a windlass (on the Calder & Hebble), and some locks where all the work is done by electricity. There are locks with handles fixed to the gear and sometimes padlocking devices to prevent unauthorized use. But the principle of raising and lowering the water-level, and then opening some kind of gate, applies everywhere.

(*above*) Gently opening a gate by leaning on the balance-beam

(*below*) Closing a lock gate as the boat leaves

An unusual way of opening a paddle on the Calder & Hebble

There is always one final thing to remember when working a lock. When the boat leaves at last, all the paddles should be fully closed, and the gates as well. This ensures that the lock remains usable, and the canal stays navigable.

7 MORE ABOUT LOCKS

Flights of Locks

The steeper the slope of a waterway, the more locks are necessary to raise and lower boats. Some canals climb quite high hills, but most locks lift a boat only about six feet. So if a waterway had to climb, say, 100 ft higher, the engineer probably built a dozen or so locks. If the slope was steep, the locks would be quite close together.

The Worcester & Birmingham Canal climbs 91 m (301 ft) in five miles along one stretch and the builders used 42 locks to raise the boats. The Leeds & Liverpool Canal at Wigan has 23 locks in about two miles, lifting or lowering boats 65 m (214 ft). Thus the broad Wigan locks were deeper than the narrow Worcester & Birmingham ones.

Where locks are fairly close together on slopes such as these, they are known as **a flight of locks**. Here is a list of the main flights now in use, with the number of locks in brackets:

Lapworth (25) *Stratford Canal*

Hatton (21) 'The Golden Steps to Heaven' *Grand Union Canal*

Wolverhampton (21) *Birmingham Canal Navigations*

Marple (16) *Peak Forest Canal*

Stourbridge (16) *Stourbridge Canal*

Audlem (15) *Shropshire Union Canal*

Perry Barr (13) *Birmingham Canal Navigations*

Farmers Bridge (13)   *Birmingham Canal Navigations*
Rothersthorpe (13)   *Grand Union Northampton Arm*
Bosley (12)   *Macclesfield Canal*
Tinsley (11)   *Sheffield & S. Yorkshire Navigation*
Aston (11)   *Birmingham Canal Navigations*
Rushall (9)   *Birmingham Canal Navigations*
Napton (9)   *Oxford Canal*
Walsall (8)   *Birmingham Canal Navigations*
Ryders Green (8)   *Birmingham Canal Navigations*
Delph (8)   *Birmingham Canal Navigations*
Wheelock (8) but there are 26 locks in six miles along
   here, often called 'Heartbreak Hill'   *Trent & Mersey
   Canal*
Johnson's Hillock (7)   *Leeds & Liverpool Canal*

It will be noticed that many of the flights are in the
Birmingham Canal Navigations. This area is often
thought of as the heart of the canal system, with
various canals leading to it. Being on a plateau, they
all have to climb considerably, hence the surfeit of
locks.

There are many flights of six, five, four and three
locks. A famous flight near Devizes on the Kennet &
Avon Canal has 29 locks, and these are rapidly being
restored.

Staircases

In a few places slopes are so steep that locks were built
next to each other, with no canal pound in between.
When this occurs, the gates between one lock and the
next are quite tall, being the depth of two locks. From
a boat in one of these locks the gates tower above you.
A group of locks built in this way is called a **staircase**

(*above*) The 21 Grand Union locks at Hatton in Warwickshire climb 146 ft in 2 miles

(*left*) 23 locks at Wigan on the Leeds & Liverpool climb 214 ft in 2¼ miles

The 5-lock Bingley staircase in Yorkshire, seen from the 3-lock staircase which precedes it

or **riser**. There is a famous staircase of five locks at Bingley in Yorkshire, on the Leeds & Liverpool Canal, and a number of others of three or two locks on the same canal nearby. These are broad locks.

There are narrow-lock staircases on the Grand Union Leicester Line at Foxton (two staircases of five locks each), and at Watford in Northamptonshire (a staircase of four locks and three ordinary locks). Pairs of staircase locks have been built at several other places, but the greatest staircase in Britain is on the Caledonian Canal in Scotland, where eight big locks are built next to each other at Banavie. Large fishing boats use this canal, as well as pleasure boats. It also has other staircases, including Fort Augustus (5) and Muirtown (4).

Working through the locks in a staircase raises problems. When you open the paddles of one lock

The intermediate gates at Bingley look massive from a boat in the lock below

the water must usually run down into the lock below. If this is full, the water will flood over the sides. This sometimes happens if people are not thinking, for of course the lower lock should have been emptied in readiness. Sometimes, however, **side-ponds** are provided, and the water runs in and out of these instead. In other places there are overflows at the lock-edges, so that if too much water is flowing into a lock it can run away in the overflow and down a channel into the canal below the staircase.

Staircase locks are interesting places to visit, and Foxton and Bingley attract many spectators in summer. Once a boat is in a staircase on a narrow canal no boat can move the opposite way in those locks until the first one has cleared them all. In a staircase of broad locks it is possible for two narrow boats to pass each other in opposite directions, though this looks odd.

The following are the staircases now in use:

Banavie (8) *Caledonian Canal*
Fort Augustus (5) *Caledonian Canal*
Bingley Five-Rise (5) *Leeds & Liverpool Canal*
Foxton (two groups of 5 each) *Grand Union Leicester Line*
Watford (4) *Grand Union Leicester Line*
Muirtown (4) *Caledonian Canal*
Chester (3) *Shropshire Union Canal*
Grindley Brook (3) *Llangollen Canal*
Newlay (3) *Leeds & Liverpool Canal*
Forge (3) *Leeds & Liverpool Canal*
Field (3) *Leeds & Liverpool Canal*
Bingley Three-Rise (3) *Leeds & Liverpool Canal*
Oddy (2) *Leeds & Liverpool Canal*
Dobsons (2) *Leeds & Liverpool Canal*
Dowley Gap (2) *Leeds & Liverpool Canal*
Stourport (two groups of 2 each) *Staffs & Worcs Canal (basin)*
Bascote (2) *Grand Union Canal*
Marsworth (2) *Grand Union Aylesbury Arm*
Etruria (2) *Caldon Canal*
Bunbury (2) *Shropshire Union*
Brades (2) *Birmingham Canal Navigations*
Laggan (2) *Caledonian Canal*

There are also three locks with very short pounds between them at The Bratch on the *Staffs & Worcs Canal*, and two similar ones on the *Stourbridge Canal*.

A 2-lock narrow-canal staircase on the Caldon Canal

Many lock footbridges are in this style on the Leeds & Liverpool Canal

Footbridges

At all locks there must be some way for people to cross over from one side to the other to work the lock. If there is a road bridge, this may be used, but very many locks are not near to roads. Thus there is often a special footbridge, and many different designs for these have been created.

On the Leeds & Liverpool there are solid wooden bridges with handrails. On the Staffs & Worcs there are decorated metal ones. The staircases at Watford and Foxton have another wooden type with rails, and in Chester there are some fine metal ones with railings. At Bosley on the Macclesfield there are also decorative metal footbridges. In other places narrow wooden bridges without railings may be found, but

(above) Decorative lock-crossing on the Staffs & Worcs Canal

(below) Simple Trent & Mersey lock footbridge

A variety of
footbridges, both
wooden and metal

81

Split footbridge on the Trent & Mersey enabling the horse's towline to pass through

at many locks there are no separate footbridges at all. Instead you cross on footplanks fastened to the lock-gates, usually with a rail to hold on to.

Some of the most interesting footbridges have slits in them, like the farm bridges on the Stratford Canal mentioned on p. 48. When all boats were pulled by animals the rope went through the slit, so that it wasn't necessary to unfasten it. You can see such gaps in many footbridges on the Trent & Mersey north of Stoke-on-Trent and at some of the locks on the Staffs & Worcs Canal.

Bollards, Steps, Ladders and Weirs

Many locks have **bollards** both alongside the lock itself and by the towpath above and below the lock. These are posts of wood, metal or concrete to which boats can be moored with their ropes. Tying a boat prevents it from drifting away, or moving backwards or forwards in a lock. But a boat going down in a

A boat roped to a bollard

lock must not be tied tightly. Sometimes people pass a rope round a bollard and back to the boat, so that someone on the boat can let it out slowly as the boat gradually goes lower down.

Look for **steps** also. These may have been provided for boaters to get down the slope from the lockside to the pound down below. Sometimes they are straight and steep, or they may curve round from the end of a balance-beam, or they may be in the curved wall down from the lock. Deep locks may have **ladders** in their side-walls, so that people can climb on and off their boats. They are also useful if anyone falls in the lock, but it is quite difficult climbing a vertical ladder.

Alongside many locks there are **weirs**, or **by-washes**. These are water-channels to carry surplus water from one pound to the next. Sometimes, as at many locks on the Northampton Arm of the Grand

Steps down from a lock near Stone in Staffordshire

Union Canal, the water runs in an open channel. On the Leeds & Liverpool, and also along the Llangollen Canal, there are some quite swift weirs. On some canals the water runs underground round the lock. The Staffs & Worcs Canal has some unusual weirs with a framework at the top end to catch branches and other rubbish before the water goes underground. The water from weirs comes out into the next pound just below the lock. Sometimes it is so close to the lock that it twists boats a little as they are moving in and out.

(*above*) Fast flowing weir on the Llangollen. Unlike most canals, water actually flows down this one to feed reservoirs

(*below*) Unusual circular weir found on the Staffs & Worcs. The water runs underground to below the lock

Striking barrel-roofed lock-house on the Stratford, seen past one of that canal's split-bridges

The weirs on rivers, of course, are the river-channel itself, and are quite wide to allow the river to keep flowing past its locks. On some rivers the weir-stream may be well away from the locks, with short canal-cuts leading to and from the locks.

Lock-keepers and Lock-cottages

In their commercial heyday the canals had lock-keepers living in cottages by the locks, to look after the locks and paddle-gear, and to help boats through. At some places there were also toll-keepers to collect tolls for the various canals. Nowadays boat-owners buy comprehensive licences instead, so there are toll-keepers only on one or two rivers. There are not many lock-keepers either, though a few remain at locks on some rivers, especially where the locks have been electrified.

Lock cottages, like the locks themselves, were built in different styles on different waterways. Many have now been pulled down as they were so isolated, but you can often find lilac bushes or rose trees, indicating where a garden has been. Sometimes the houses have been saved and bought by people who are waterway enthusiasts. There are several of these on the southern Stratford Canal, with unusual rounded roofs.

The remaining lock-keepers on the smaller canals live at some of the most important lock-flights. On commercial canals such as the Aire & Calder Navigation there is a keeper at each lock, with a house and also a lock-cabin where he can see the boats and control the lock electrically. Other keepers man apparatus on the Thames, Trent and Severn.

Lifts and Slopes

Any study of the history of waterway locks soon reveals that men were always trying to invent other ways of raising and lowering boats. Over 100 years ago there were eight **lifts** for boats on a canal in Somerset, taking them up and down in tanks of water. There were several other experiments with lifts of different kinds.

Another way of raising boats was by putting them into a large tank fitted with wheels and pulling the tank up a slope. Such inclined planes existed in Shropshire, in Cornwall and in Scotland, and formerly one was used instead of the Foxton staircase locks. This was closed because it was too expensive to keep

Approaching the Anderton boat-lift from the river Weaver.
The Trent & Mersey Canal runs above

steam engines working while awaiting boats. Parts of
this plane near the locks can still be seen. An enormous
inclined plane was built quite recently in Europe
which will lift great barges 67 m (320 ft) up a hillside.

The Anderton Lift near Northwich, alongside the
Trent & Mersey Canal, is a famous boat-lift unique
in this country. It has been closed for some time, but
hopefully will be open again shortly. Boats from the
canal move along a short trough into this lift and are
then lowered 15 m (just over 50 ft) to the level of
the river Weaver. It has two parallel tanks with
guillotine gates at the ends to keep the water in.
Other gates seal off the canal and the river. Boats are
lowered or raised in a few minutes on the end of
long cables, running over many pulleys at the top of
the structure.

8   BOATS AND BOATMEN

In early times many of the river boats used sails, but
these boats could rarely be used on the narrower
canals, even if they fitted the locks. There were also
many bridges to impede sails, so canal boats usually
had to be towed. Boats on rivers had sometimes been
pulled along by gangs of men, or by horses or mules,
pushing their way through the trees and bushes on
the banks. Special towing paths were made alongside
canals for the towing animals to walk on. These
towpaths make pleasant walks nowadays.

The canal boats were towed by means of a long
rope fixed to a post part-way along the boat. If the
post had been right at the front, the boat would
constantly be pulled towards the bank. Because the

A horse towing a boat

A Leeds & Liverpool Canal 'short boat'. Many have been
converted as cruising boats

post was further back, the steerer was more easily able
to keep the boat moving in the deeper channel.

There were boats of many different shapes and sizes
using the new waterways in different parts of the
country.

Barges

Wider boats, usually called barges, used the rivers and
the broad canals, and there were as many as 200
different kinds. Bridgewater Canal barges were about
68 ft by 14 ft (20.7 m by 4.27 m) at one time, and
later when locks were made bigger they were 88 ft
by 15 ft (26.82 m by 4.57 m). On the Leeds &
Liverpool Canal the barges were often called **short
boats** because of the shorter locks there. They were
about 60 ft by 14 ft (18.29 m by 4.27 m), but there
were much bigger barges on rivers such as the Thames
and Severn, and all sorts of designs and sizes on other
rivers and broad canals.

(*above*) Barge at Thorne on the Sheffield & South
Yorkshire Navigation

(*below*) Unloading a sand-barge at Knottingley on the
Aire & Calder Navigation

There are many coal-barges in Yorkshire. This one is approaching the lock at Ferrybridge

Barges can still be found on all our remaining commercial waterways, carrying coal, oil, gravel, timber, grain, effluent, etc., and examples of different types can be seen in many places, especially at the Boat Museum at Ellesmere Port.

Narrow Boats

The narrow locks on the canals in the central parts of the country were only 7 ft wide and 70 ft long (2.13 m by 21.34 m), so special boats were built for these canals. These should correctly be called **narrow boats**, though they too are often wrongly referred to as 'barges'.

They have also been called **monkey boats** and **long boats**. Again there have been many different types of vessel and enthusiasts can tell at a glance the type of boat, its builder, and the special purpose (or

Now a rare sight. A pair of narrow boats (the 'motor' towing the 'butty') carrying cargo on the Grand Union Canal

canal) for which it was built. This, even though many of the old ones have now had cabins built on to the original hulls to convert them to pleasure craft.

Many of the early narrow boats were **day boats**, making short journeys in such areas as the Birmingham canals. But in time, as boats travelled over the growing network of canals, small cabins were built on the back for the boatman to live in.

These were ingeniously designed, and when you think that in later years a man and his wife and family lived in them, it is astonishing how everything and everybody could get into such a small space. The cabin might be only 10 ft by 6 ft (3.05 m by 1.83 m), and just over 5 ft (1.52 m) high. There was a stove, folding beds, cupboard doors which made into tables, and beautifully-kept ornaments, crockery, curtains, and all the possessions of the family. Children were

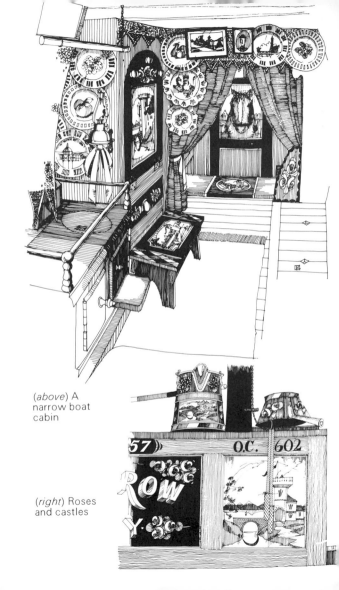

(above) A narrow boat cabin

(right) Roses and castles

born in these cabins, and boatmen and their wives died in them, for this was their only home. The cabins had to be small so that the boats could carry as much cargo as possible in the rest of the space. You can see a cabin in the Waterways Museum at Stoke Bruerne.

Even the general-purpose narrow boats were built in slightly differing shapes at different boatyards on different canals, according to the ideas of the particular builders. Then there were specially-designed boats for carrying such loads as tar and oil. The enthusiast has to be well versed in the shapes of hulls, cabins, cargo-compartments, and the curves of bows and sterns, as well as in the materials used for building, and the well-known boatyards and canal companies which produced the boats.

Different types of boats may be known by boatyard names, or by nicknames, with connoisseurs talking avidly about **Joshers**, **Joeys**, **Darlow Boats**, **Northwich Boats**, **Large Woolwich** and **Small Woolwich**, etc.

Many narrow boats were owned by large companies which carried goods on canals and rivers, but many were also owned by boatmen known as **Number Ones**, who carried cargoes for any trader.

Perhaps the most interesting aspect of the narrow boats was the painted decoration on them, and this can still be seen today, both on the few cargo narrow boats still operating and on the many more which have been turned into pleasure boats. The traditional decoration uses designs of roses and castles, with a few colourful geometrical shapes. The roses and castles appear everywhere – on boat-sides, doors, water-cans, lamps, feeding-bowls for the horses, and even on

95

curtains and stools. Yet no-one is sure why roses and castles are used. Unhappily, much trashy material is sold along canals today with poor attempts at reproducing the same designs.

The boats also had many pieces of brass on lamps and chimneys, and on the horses' harness, and boatmen used to weave ropes in pleasant shapes to decorate the tiller. Sometimes the tail of a dead canal horse would hang from the tiller-post.

Other Boats

In addition to the more common barges and narrow boats, there were boats of other shapes and sizes. On the Aire & Calder Navigation, and in a few other places, small **compartment boats** were pulled in trains. These were used until quite recently on the Aire & Calder. They were affectionately called **Tom Puddings** and were oblong iron boxes towed behind a tug. They were lifted out of the water at the port of Goole, and the lift tipped them up to shoot their cargo of coal into ocean-going ships.

The Duke of Bridgewater used certain small boats nicknamed **starvationers** to bring coal out of the underground canals in his mines and on to the Bridgewater Canal. They were about 50 ft by just over 4 ft (15.24 m by 1.22 m). On some small coal canals – for example in Shropshire and Somerset – small box-shaped **tub-boats** were used. They too sometimes travelled in trains, and some on the Bude Canal had wheels, for they ran on rails on a slope from one canal level to another.

Fly-boats were rather like the expresses of the canals. They had priority over other traffic and, in some places, would run through the night. They carried parcels and passengers, and were pulled by relays of horses at speeds as great as ten mph. The horses were changed every few miles.

In any study of boats you will come across various other types of vessels. There are several kinds of **tugs** and **dredgers**, for example, used both in the past and nowadays. **Maintenance boats**, both broad and narrow, work along the waterways, with engineless **hoppers** being used to remove mud and rubbish taken out of the water.

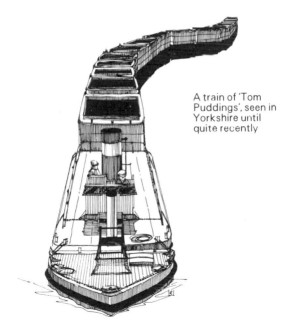

A train of 'Tom Puddings', seen in Yorkshire until quite recently

(*above*)
There are
not enough
dredgers on
canals. Here
is one of
them on the
Trent &
Mersey

(*right*)
Maintenance
men and
boat at work
– in this case
replacing a
dislodged
lock-side
stone

Cargoes

It must be remembered that in the first days of canals they were the chief means of transport. Boats carried many of the heavy cargoes which lorries and trains do today. Coal was one of the main loads and was taken from mines to the factories which were springing up everywhere. But all kinds of other cargoes were carried. Here is a list of some, taken from canal records of the past:

stone	woad	vinegar	shoes
manure	cloth	sugar	pipes
timber	slate	cider	wool
rags	corn	leather	lead
bricks	tea	lime	cheese
hops	soap	gravel	paper

Boats would take a load from one place to another, and then carry different goods for the return journey. Often the boatman had to clean out the boat after a dirty load ready for a clean one.

Some boats, such as the fly-boats, also carried passengers. Water-travel was much more peaceful and smoother than travel in stage coaches, and there would be trips to a nearby market-town or even to the races. In Scotland, there were boats between Glasgow and Edinburgh which had sleeping compartments; passenger-boats in many places had superior sections for the richer people and less comfortable seats for the others. In 1835, for example, nearly 400,000 passengers travelled on a canal between Glasgow and Paisley, with twelve boats running each way daily. Many other canals ran passenger journeys before the days of the railway.

Engines

When steam engines were invented, they were obviously suitable for driving boats. It seems that they were first tried on the Forth & Clyde Canal, but steam engines came into common use on rivers some time before they appeared widely on canals. The canal companies feared – with some justification – that steam-driven boats would damage the banks with the water washed about by their paddle-wheels. And in fact powered boats are even now the chief cause of bank damage.

However, 'steamers' soon appeared almost everywhere, more often using propellers by then instead of paddle-wheels. The engines took up a lot of space, not to mention the coke or coal for their boilers. Thus the cargoes carried could not be as large as in the horse-drawn boats.

Eventually engines driven by diesel oil came into use about 50 years ago. These engines take up less space than steam engines, so there was again more room for cargo. The noise of a diesel engine in a narrow boat is one of the distinctive canal noises even today, and its 'chug-chug' sounds surprisingly pleasant coming towards you from the distance. Enthusiasts almost weep at the sound of one of the early engines.

Most barges and narrow boats now – including pleasure boats – use diesel engines. Smaller pleasure boats may have petrol engines, or small 'outboard engines' fixed on the back, running on a mixture of petrol and oil.

An interesting sight is a pair of narrow boats travelling together. They may be cargo boats, or they may be camping boats for young people, or **hotel**

boats, taking about twelve holiday-makers in small cabins. When two narrow boats cruise together in this way, one has no engine. This is called the **butty**, while the one with the engine is called the **motor**. The latter usually tows the butty, but the two boats can also be roped together side by side if the canal is wide enough. They are also roped together in this way when going into broad locks, where they just fit.

Boat People

Nobody is quite sure where the canal boat people first came from, but it is probably not true to say that they were gipsies. They were certainly very proud people – especially those Number Ones who had their own boats and did not work for a company. Boat people knew each other up and down the canals, even though they met rarely. They married among themselves,

A pair of narrow boats

and left messages for each other at locks and pubs, and usually they took a great pride in their cabins and their best clothes. You can see some of these clothes in the Waterways Museum, and also many photographs of the people, both in their working dress and in 'walking out' dress.

The bargees on the rivers and some broad canals were thought to be a quite different kind of people who originally came from the sea and the river estuaries. It is the boatmen on the narrow boats who are such an interesting study.

Their lives were often hard. They were working in all weathers, especially after competition from the railways began. They lived in very crowded conditions, and the children were unable to go to school. Undoubtedly some of the boatmen were rough, making their children work at quite an early age. One inspector found 167 children on 96 boats, and many of them worked by driving the horse, steering the boat, and opening and shutting heavy lock-gates. One 13-year-old boy, driving a horse, had been working all night. The boatman's wife would steer the boat while carrying a small baby, even in rain and snow; everyone worked long hours for little money.

In time, people became concerned about conditions on the narrow boats and especially about the children. In 1877 a Canal Boats Act was passed, in an attempt to make life easier for these people. Inspections of boats took place, and later on schools were set up at strategic places on the canals.

Nowadays there are few if any boats with families living on them. The remaining narrow boats which carry goods are often worked by young people who like the life. The days are over when thousands of cargo boats were also homes to large families.

Cargo-carrying Today

The big canal companies carrying goods on the narrow canals have disappeared because roads and railways have taken their trade. The groups of people running such boats cannot make much money, for the boats hold so little compared with barges, and compared especially with the large barges on the big canals of Europe. Unhappily our narrow canals have become so shallow and filled with rubbish that the boats cannot even be fully loaded.

Even so, in recent years some narrow boats have continued to carry coal and even cargoes of bicycles,

An oil tanker barge on the Aire & Calder

oil, timber and stone have been seen. Lime juice in drums recently came up the Grand Union, and the enthusiasts who run these boats are always on the lookout for cargoes. But the real need is for larger canals and locks, to take much bigger boats.

The main trade now is on the rivers and some broad canals, where the barges can take more economical loads. You will see timber, for example, going up the river Lee, gravel and oil on the Trent and on the Aire & Calder, and coal for power stations in Yorkshire, as well as cargoes to Rotherham.

The ship canals and rivers still serve a useful purpose. Sea-going vessels reach Manchester on the Ship Canal, and others use the river Weaver and the Gloucester & Sharpness Ship Canal; smaller boats pass through the Caledonian and Crinan Canals in Scotland.

Recently a new type of water transport has appeared on Yorkshire waterways. This is a short train of barges pushed along by what is called (curiously) a **push-tug**, driven by one man. Push-tugs take these large compartment-boats full of coal from collieries to power stations; the containers are much larger than the Tom Puddings. The containers (also called 'pans') are lifted out of the water at power stations and emptied onto conveyor belts, rather as the Tom Puddings' contents were tipped into ships at Goole.

The most promising idea with push-tugs, however, was to take trains of container-shaped barges, loaded with all kinds of goods, to a port. There they were lifted out of the water on to a 'mother-ship' to cross the Channel, or even the Atlantic. They were

(*above*)
Unusual
encounter –
canal boat and
sea-going ship
in a lock at
Goole, about
to enter the
Yorkshire
Ouse. Ships
use some
rivers, as well
as two ship
canals

(*left*) More
modern
'compart-
ment-boats',
filled with
coal and
being
pushed by a
tug to
Ferrybridge
power
stations in
Yorkshire

then transferred to a river or canal and pushed to their destination. Thus the goods in them never had to be unpacked from start to finish, like the containers taken by road and rail. But the waterborne containers were much larger and infinitely less costly to handle. Unfortunately dock unions put a stop to this idea and it had to be abandoned.

Britain is only just beginning to think of ideas such as this, but the system is widely used in America and continental Europe. In order to compete, we need a vast enlargement programme for our existing canals, and new canals also. Other countries in Europe are constantly enlarging and digging, knowing the enormous fuel-saving potential. We should be developing our canals for cross-Channel transport in the same way.

9 USING CANALS FOR LEISURE

Although canals were first dug, and rivers improved, in order to carry goods all over the country, they are little used for this purpose nowadays. However much we should be developing our canals for goods, the fact is that they are mostly used for leisure – boating, angling, walking, bird-watching, flower-identifying, and so on.

In summer especially, many people enjoy themselves in boats, but there are many more who also get pleasure from canals, merely by sitting beside them. Because of this new wide leisure use, further lengths of waterway are still being restored – often by volunteers – for the general enjoyment of others.

Pleasure Boats

People can travel in all kinds of boats on waterways, from canoes to large motor cruisers which provide necessary accommodation for families to live, sleep and eat for weeks at a time. There are inflatables, rowing-boats, open boats with small engines, small cruisers with cabins, and the much larger cruising boats, some converted from former commercial boats, but most with hulls specially built to the same shape as those of the commercial boats. Many of these latter boats are shown in photographs throughout this book, which often include the boat belonging to the author.

(*above*) Sea-going yachts taking the short cut through the Crinan Canal in Scotland

(*right*) Canoeists often use canals, at a low licence rate

Plan of a holiday cruising boat

Most of the boats you see have been hired for a holiday and are likely to be travelling for a week or a fortnight. Some of the beds aboard have been cunningly designed to convert into a table and seats during the day, and there will be wash-basins, a cooker, often a refrigerator and shower, as well as electric light run from batteries. The cooker runs on bottled gas, and the water available on the boat is carried in water-tanks or containers which are filled from taps along the waterways. Above is a plan of a typical 'narrow boat' holiday cruiser.

Such boats are virtually floating homes and often very comfortable. The term 'narrow boat' is strictly used for the commercial boats of the narrow canals, as we saw earlier, but it has come to be widely used for the steel-hulled holiday boats so common now. Those owners who have converted a genuine old narrow boat tend to look down on modern versions, and even to object to their being called narrow boats.

The commercial boats used to be built of wood, but most smaller cruisers now are made of 'glass reinforced plastic' – GRP for short, often called 'fibreglass'. This can be quite strong and resistant to bumps, but care is needed at locks. The bigger narrow boats, as already mentioned, are usually built of steel nowadays.

For those who would rather not hire a holiday boat, there are pleasant **hotel boats** cruising, with

(*right*) Small pleasure cruiser with a fibre-glass hull

(*far right, above*) Hotel boats

(*below*) Steel-hulled hire-boat

(*far right, below*) Short-trip boat

III

A 'marina' by the Grand Union Canal at Whilton, Northants

small cabins, dining room, etc. And all over the canals there are **trip boats** offering daytime cruises.

Besides the normal engines using petrol or diesel, more and more boats are trying out electric motors. Outboard engines use a mixture of petrol and oil. Smaller boats are steered by a spoked wheel, which turns either a rudder at the back or the whole outboard engine. Narrow boats are steered in the old way by a tiller at the back moving a rudder under water.

Where the Boats come from

Many of the boats seen on canals are hired, and there are hire-bases all over our waterway system. It is often necessary to book a boat months beforehand, or there may be little choice left. Boats come in all shapes and sizes. Everything is provided except the food you need, so you just arrive at the boatyard and step aboard as if moving into a small house. If you have never steered a boat before someone will show you

Hire cruisers at a base at Great Haywood, Staffs

how, and he should also show you how to go through a lock. After that you are free to travel wherever you like, so long as you are back in time at the end of the holiday.

People wishing to buy their own boat have many places to choose from. There are boatbuilders who will build a boat to meet your exact requirements, and other firms make large numbers of standard boats of various kinds. At places along canals and rivers – or even away from them – you can examine the different types available.

Boatyards on waterways are rather like garages on roads. They carry out repairs, or fill up tanks with fuel. Some yards are just at the side of the water and

Boats moored along the Oxford Canal

there is little room for boats. Others have areas of water for the permanent mooring of vessels. These may be former canal basins or reservoirs, or they may have been dug out especially from a field at the side of the waterway. They are often called **marinas** – a curious word for inland waters, since it refers to the sea. A better name is **harbours**.

Not all boats are kept in harbours or even at boatyards, and you will see them moored casually along the banks. Some people have a house near the bank of a canal and keep their boat at the bottom of the garden.

As with roads, you need a licence to take a boat on almost every inland waterway. One licence from the British Waterways Board covers nearly every canal and several rivers such as the Trent, Severn, Weaver and Soar. But two or three canals, and several rivers, come under other bodies, and you must have different licences in order to use them. These include the Thames, Wey, Nene, Great Ouse, Yorkshire Ouse, Warwickshire Avon, Bridgewater Canal and Southern Stratford Canal.

It is, therefore, usually illegal to put a boat into the water – even a canoe – without paying towards the high cost of maintaining banks, bridges, locks, tunnels, aqueducts, and the many other parts of the waterway which need constant maintenance.

Cruising

Once you are in a boat, with its correct licence, you can cruise where you wish. Boats pass each other in the opposite way to cars – moving over to the right. Steering is quite different, too, for a boat isn't firmly on the water as a car is on the road, and even the wind will move it sideways. Steering through narrow bridge-openings and into locks is quite difficult until you get used to it.

Moving through locks is the most energetic part of cruising. Some people enjoy the exercise of locking, and they will take their boats to places where they know there are hills and therefore many locks.

As you can see from the map on p. 156, there are many hundreds of miles where people can cruise, and quite varied routes can be planned. You can stop where you like, either in the middle of the country or

(*above*) Moored below a pub on the Stratford Canal

(*below*) Rural mooring between Wigan and Blackburn on the Leeds & Liverpool Canal

Cruising amid 24 locks into the heart of Birmingham, yet curiously remote

A peaceful view from the Ashby Canal

near a village or a town. Canals may go for miles without actually passing through villages or towns, but there is usually a village not far away.

Care is needed sometimes to moor a boat, since the canal sides may be shallow, but you can usually reach the towpath somewhere. There, you have to knock in strong metal pegs, called **mooring-pins**, for tying up the bows and stern of the boat. Boats shouldn't be moored on bends, or near locks or narrow bridges.

You will need to do some shopping for food, of course, and there are often interesting village shops, and sometimes even local types of food. You will also need to stop at water-taps to fill the tanks on your vessel, and perhaps at a boatyard for fuel. Then there

The Regent's Canal in London passes through the Zoo,
with a boat's eye view of Lord Snowdon's aviary

are places along waterways for emptying the special
kinds of lavatories used on board.

Boats travel very slowly, especially on shallow
canals, and there is normally a speed limit of 4 mph.
This sounds extremely slow, but it does make it
possible to look around in a way unknown on a road.
If there are any locks, you rarely travel much more
than twenty miles in a day. It's astonishing, though,
how full a day can seem. You are so busy doing
something, looking around, walking in a nearby
village, scraping over an aqueduct, identifying birds
or flowers, sunbathing, or just mooring and starting
off again, that at the end of a day you can barely
remember what happened at the beginning. It is

certainly a very enjoyable and peaceful way of spending a holiday.

Fishing

There are certain times of the year when fishing is not allowed on inland waterways. During most of the summer, however, you will see anglers along every canal and river, especially at weekends. They belong to one of the many angling clubs, or they may have paid a small sum for a day's fishing. They bring along rods, lines, hooks, bait, stool, umbrella and keep-net for a day in the fresh air. Many children enjoy fishing, and though people seem to catch only small fish in canals, this is their sport, and they put all the fish back in the water at the end of the day.

Unfortunately, along narrow canals, anglers and boaters may be in each other's way. Boats may need to keep near the middle to avoid going aground, and this is just where the anglers want to catch their fish.

A canal angler

Week-end angling match on the Grand Union Canal in Buckinghamshire

Anglers may also wish to fish near locks, because this seems a good place for fish; but of course boats have to moor there in order to operate the lock.

Anglers usually pull out their lines when a boat appears, and boaters should slow down and keep away from anglers as much as possible. When there is a fishing match at weekends, there may be hundreds of fishermen stretching for miles along the bank. Most people try to be helpful to each other along waterways, so that they can enjoy themselves in their own way.

Anglers are knowledgeable about rivers and canals, and usually know just where to seek various kinds of fish, and the best bait to use at different places and times. Unhappily the waters are not always as clean and clear as they ought to be because of the poisons and other material coming into them from factories and fields. This is bad for the fish, but it is not always easy to catch anyone allowing poisonous waste to pollute a waterway.

10   ALONG THE WATERWAYS

Whether you look at waterways from bridges, towpaths and banks, or travel along them in a boat, there are many fascinating things to see. Some are the living and growing things both in and around the water. Others are the buildings, bridges, mileposts, bollards and other items which the makers of the waterway installed.

Many have already been mentioned in various connections. Certainly there is hardly a moment when there is not something to catch your eye, and often it is worth examining more closely. It is impossible to list everything that you might see, but this chapter gives a selection of items worth looking for.

Locks and Paddle-gear

There is a great variety of paddle-gear. When exploring a canal look for ground-paddles and gate-paddles, for paddles which pull upwards and paddles which move sideways, and for different kinds of gears (including the new hydraulic type being fitted at some locks). Try to find great wooden balance-beams and ugly little metal ones, bent beams and beams made of telegraph poles. There are even gates which have no beams at all (some on the river Lee have to be opened and closed by ropes). Watch out for single lock gates and pairs of gates, and sills against which the top gates rest (the bottom sills don't emerge from

(*above*) Here and there, balance-beams have been
cranked to allow for road widenings. This is a deep lock
out of Stourport Basin

(*below*) An unusual method of opening a lock-gate, on
the Lee Navigation

(*far left, above*) Simple lock footbridge with a slit for the tow-rope

(*above*) Ladder in a lock-side

(*far left, below*) Steps down from the end of a lock

(*left*) 'Distance post' on the Oxford Canal

the water). Note various kinds of foot-crossings, and the steps below many locks for the crew to get back on their boat.

You will find weirs at the side of many locks, to take spare water from the pound above to the pound below. Look out for ladders in the sides of some deep locks so that people can climb on and off their boats, or use them to rescue someone who has fallen into an empty lock. Perhaps you will notice deep grooves cut by ropes along lock-edges or over balance-beams, from the days when boats were towed. You may also find little hooks for towing-ropes at many locks on the Worcester & Birmingham Canal, and 'lock-distance' posts on the Grand Union, Oxford and river Weaver. These posts are found a little way before the lock; a boat reaching the post first had the right to the lock.

You may be able to see electrically-worked locks on the river Thames, the lower Lee, the Aire & Calder, the Severn and the Manchester Ship Canal. These are quite intriguing, though maybe not as interesting as the locks which are worked by boat crews themselves.

Bridges, Tunnels and Aqueducts

Bridges vary greatly in shape, even along one waterway. Some types are different because they are built by different companies. If a bridge is on a bend you will almost certainly find rope-grooves on its corners. You may also find metal posts which were often fixed to corners to protect them from ropes. Even the metal posts have deep cuts in them.

(*above*) Tow-rope grooves in a bridge corner near Wolverhampton

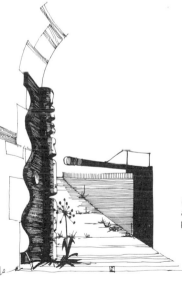

(*left*) Rope grooves on a metal post protecting a bridge

127

Graceful towpath bridge in Birmingham

Study the various types of footbridges, and the towpath bridges which took the horses over branches or other canals, or took them across the canal when the path changed sides. Look out for the split bridges on some canals which were made for the towrope to pass. Remember, too, the lifting and swinging bridges, both the small ones which crews work for themselves on the narrow canals, and the larger ones which are worked by electricity on broad canals and rivers. If you can visit the swinging aqueduct at Barton it is a remarkable sight to see a box full of water opening to allow the Manchester Ship Canal giant vessels to pass by below.

Aqueducts and tunnels are not so easy to find, but there is Blisworth tunnel near to the Waterways Museum (which itself is of course an essential visit). Most canals have at least a small aqueduct in the vicinity, even if you cannot reach the great Pontcysyllte in North Wales. The Edstone aqueduct north of

(*above*) An unusual lift-bridge at Huddersfield. The whole bridge rises into the air at the turning of a handle

(*below*) Modern electric lift-bridge on the Gloucester & Sharpness Ship Canal

(*above*) Short and narrow tunnel on the Birmingham and Fazeley

(*below*) Surprising aqueduct at Wootten Wawen, over the busy Birmingham-Stratford road

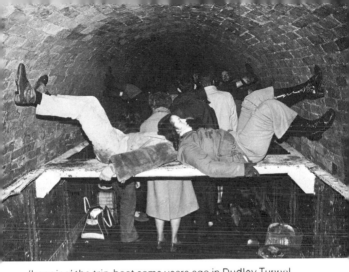

'Legging' the trip-boat some years ago in Dudley Tunnel

Stratford-upon-Avon is impressive; the smaller one taking the canal over the Birmingham to Stratford road at Wootten Wawen is often unnoticed by people on the road.

Whenever a canal is on a high embankment you are likely to find small aqueducts, either where a canal crosses over a stream or where it passes over a road. The great embankments of the Shropshire Union Canal often cross streams and roads, and at times the boats there float along above the chimney-tops of houses nearby.

Sometimes there are trip-boats through tunnels. A small narrow boat called *Charlie* takes passengers through Blisworth tunnel, and you may visit part of the famous tunnel at Dudley.

Mileposts, Bollards and Stop-planks

As you explore a waterway you will often see small items on the bank. Canals had **mileposts** so that tolls charged for carrying goods could be assessed; many of these posts can still be found, even if you have to poke among nettles. Those on the Leeds & Liverpool Canal are more like road milestones, but the Trent & Mersey has some pleasantly-shaped ones, and so has the Shropshire Union. There are a number along the Grand Union, too, and on the river Medway there are some old stone ones with Roman numerals. The ones on the Monmouthshire & Brecon Canal just have numbers, with no place names.

Bollards (see p. 82) are the wooden, concrete or metal posts necessary for tying up boats. You may moor your boat in this way while you shop or stay the night, or merely use bollards at locks to stop the boat from moving about too much. Sometimes, on quays, there are metal rings instead.

Many of the old wooden bollards have rotted away, and any that remain are likely to be very worn, with deep rope-grooves. Even some of the heavy metal bollards – at Wigan, for example – may have rope-grooves in the metal. There are large metal ones on the river Nene, and even bigger ones for the sea-going ships on the Gloucester & Sharpness Ship Canal and the river Weaver. The Lee not only has bollards along the top edges of the locks, but also some set into the lock-walls by the water.

Some canals have bollards both alongside the locks and just above and below them, for tying up a boat while preparing the lock for use. New bollards made of concrete – which don't look as pleasant as the old

Different kinds of milepost found along the canals

Bollards

Unusual bollards are set in lock walls in several places on the river Lee

ones – have been put up in recent years for the use of pleasure boats.

Sometimes, near narrow bridges or at locks, you may see a set of thick boards. These are **stop-planks**, and if you examine the bridge or the lock you will find grooves either side of the water into which these planks can be slid, one after another, to make a dam. The waterway can then be pumped dry, or the lock emptied, in between two sets of these planks in order to repair gates, walls or banks.

If a canal bursts its banks – which occasionally happens – stop-planks must be put in quickly at narrow places on either side of the burst, to prevent the rest of the water from draining away. Stop-planks are heavy, and on broad canals such as the Bridgewater there may be a crane beside a pile of planks ready to lift them.

(*above*) Bridgewater Canal stop-planks and a crane to lift them

(*below*) Simple stop-planks on a narrow canal

Notices and Numbers

There are some unusual and even amusing notices still to be found along waterways. On the Llangollen Canal one says

BOATMEN MUST PUT THIS LIFT UP BRIDGE DOWN CAREFULLY AFTER THEIR BOAT HAS PASSED UNDER

You will find many notices on bridges, usually telling you that nothing must cross the bridge which exceeds 'the weight of the ordinary traffic of the district' (which must have changed greatly since the notice was put up!). You have probably seen the old diamond-shaped bridge notices on roads, giving the weights which the bridge will take. There are also newer notices showing the axle-weight limit of a bridge.

Nowadays you will also come across new notices at lift-bridges and swing-bridges, reminding people

A canal notice on the Shropshire Union Canal

that only genuine users of the waterway are allowed to work the bridges. Then there are notices at many water-taps telling you where the next tap is along the canal, and notices on lock-gates asking boaters to work the paddles properly. There is a notice on the Kennet & Avon Canal at Newbury which says

THE CAPTAIN OF EVERY VESSEL ALLOWING
HORSES TO HAUL ACROSS THE STREET
WILL BE FINED.
BY ORDER.

There is one at the entrance to the Fossdyke Canal forbidding boats to drag an anchor along the canal bed. But you are no longer threatened by transportation for committing offences, as a notice now at the Waterways Museum once warned.

If you poke around a bit at the sides of many canals you may find old **boundary posts**. 'MR', for the Midland Railway which once owned it, is very

A notice beside the Nottingham Canal

Various ways
of marking
boundaries,
buildings,
locks and
bridges

frequent along the Ashby Canal. You may find an
'SWC' or two along the Staffs & Worcs Canal, and
quite a number of posts along the Coventry.

There are notices about benefactors on some
Stratford Canal bollards, and similar notices at places
along the newly-restored Upper river Avon. You
may find old notices about men connected with
canals, such as the one to John Blackwell at Devizes.

Numbers on bridges are useful clues to your
whereabouts on a canal; these are in various styles,
from the bold Leeds & Liverpool ones (often blue and

white) to the rather cheaper ones put up more recently elsewhere. Some on the Trent & Mersey are carved in the bridge, and on some canals there are fine raised metal ones. The Ashby Canal bridge numbers are quite imposing.

The Staffs & Worcs Canal is well known for its bridge-plates, which have names as well as numbers. Enthusiasts have restored many of these. The Birmingham Canal Navigations also have bridge-names here and there, but no numbers. There are numbers on the lock-houses and other buildings on these Birmingham area canals.

Some locks still bear numbers, though these appear to be going out of fashion. Good solid metal ones still exist along the Llangollen and the Stratford, but the rather miserable little painted ones put on locks more recently are already fading from the balance beams.

Numbers on locks can be particularly useful where many locks come together in a flight, for they help boaters to keep count of how far they have moved along the flight. Fortunately, in the Tardebigge flight, the numbers are carved in the stone at the foot of each lock, so they should last as long as the lock does. The same applies to the great Wigan flight, and in this case Roman figures have been used.

Junctions

Places where canals join other canals or rivers are not as common as road junctions, but they are worth finding. Sometimes a signpost, like the old-fashioned tall road signposts, stands there. Some junctions can easily be missed by boaters. The entrance to the Slough Branch from the Grand Union is rather obscure, as is the important Hertford Union link from the Grand Union (Regents Canal) to the river Lee, while other junctions are quite striking places, often swarming with boats.

At Keadby, boats may have to wait in the Stainforth & Keadby Canal for the tide to turn in the river Trent down below a lock, before they can enter the river. Another interesting junction at West Stockwith on the Trent takes boats on to the isolated Chesterfield Canal (which now ends at Worksop). At Kidsgrove, in the Potteries, the Macclesfield Canal joins the Trent & Mersey after crossing over it on an aqueduct and at Trent Junction near Nottingham there is actually a waterway crossroads. The Erewash Canal comes from the north, the river Soar from the south, and the Trent runs across between them.

The Birmingham Canals are full of junctions, and you need a good map to make sure you don't take the wrong turning. At one place, the Worcester & Birmingham Canal company once refused to allow a junction to be made with the Birmingham Canal, and forced people to unload goods into its own boats. Eventually it agreed to a junction, but the place is still called Worcester Bar.

Where canals join the river Severn at Stourport and at Worcester there are large canal basins. Many boats moor there away from the river, which can be dangerous after heavy rain. There are, of course, locks between the canals and the river.

At one time, where one waterway joined another there would be a toll-house, and a narrow place – or even a lock – where boats had to stop and be examined. The boatmen would pay tolls to the next

(*left*) Modern
signpost at
Stourton
Junction
provided by the
Staffs and
Worcs Canal
Society

(*below*) On the
right is the
junction
between the
Worcester and
Birmingham
Canal and the
river Severn, at
Worcester

(*above*) Stop lock where the Shropshire Union Canal
joins the Staffs and Worcs

(*below*) An old toll-
house near
Birmingham

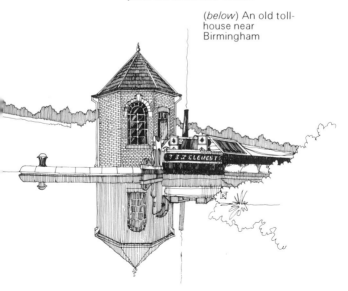

company according to the cargo and its weight. You can still see such **stop locks** at Autherley Junction, Hall Green Junction, Hawkesbury Junction and Kings Norton Junction (among others), and the first three named still have locks which raise and lower a boat only a few inches. These were to make sure that the water of one canal didn't run away into a rival canal.

Any large map of the waterways shows where one canal joined another, and where there are junctions with rivers or small branches.

Here, for example, is a list of the junctions along the main line of the Grand Union between the Thames and Birmingham:

Brentford, with the river Thames

Bulls Bridge, with the Paddington Branch

Cowley Peachey, with the Slough Branch

Bulbourne, with the Wendover Branch

Marsworth, with the Aylesbury Branch

Gayton, with the Northampton Branch

Norton, with the Leicester Line of the Grand Union

Braunston, with the Oxford Canal (North)

Napton, with the Oxford Canal (South)

Kingswood, with the Stratford Canal

Bordesley, with a branch to the Birmingham Canals

Salford Bridge, with the Tame Valley Canal, and the
Birmingham & Fazeley Canal (actually a waterway crossroads under the 'Spaghetti' motorway junction)

Examples of other well-known junctions, which you might like to locate, are: Preston Brook, Hurleston, Torksey, Marple, Fradley, Great Haywood, Castleford, Old Ford, Saul, Woodham, Marston, Fazeley, Stretford, Stourton, Barbridge.

One of several striking bridgekeeper's houses on the Gloucester & Sharpness Ship Canal

Buildings

When the canals were dug, many buildings of different types were erected, and some remain. Although large numbers of **lock-houses** have now gone, you can still find the patterns of different companies, ranging from small, low cottages to those with curved windows through which boats could be seen coming, and yet others – such as one at the Northampton locks – which are tall with wide roofs.

Try to see the barrel-shaped roofs of some houses on the Stratford Canal, and the round ones on the disused Thames & Severn Canal. You may also find quite new lock-houses in a few places, such as at Harlow on the river Stort and Evesham on the Warwickshire Avon.

The **bridge-keepers** on the Gloucester & Sharpness, the Aire & Calder, and a few other canals, also

146

Solid lock-house on the Lee Navigation

have their houses. There are no longer the toll-keepers mentioned earlier, but a few little **toll-houses** remain and some odd, round lock-watchers' huts can be seen near Chester.

There used to be numerous **warehouses** along waterways for storing goods, but many have gone. Some can still be located, even if they are now used for something else, at places such as Shardlow, Ellesmere, Stourport and Gloucester.

There are also **maintenance yards** along canals. You will find these yards all over the system, at such places as Bulls Bridge at Southall, Fradley on the Trent & Mersey, Gayton near Northampton, Hillmorton near Rugby, Bulbourne near Tring, Loughborough, Marple and Wigan. At these yards there may be workshops (perhaps making lock gates), offices, and also maintenance boats and dredgers –

147

(*above*) British Waterways Board maintenance yard at Hartshill on the Coventry Canal

(*below*) Timber for new lock gates at the Bulbourne maintenance yard near Tring

though most of these will be at work on the waterways.

Waterway Pubs

Along the canals in the busy days there were inns for the boatmen. They would usually call there for a drink, but if there was no living-cabin on their boat they might stay for the night. Some inns had stabling for the towing-horses. Today there are fewer of these pubs, but they still remain on most waterways, especially near to bridges where they can be used now by motorists, as well as boaters, walkers and anglers. Most have 'watery' names such as *Boat*, *Wharf*, *Navigation*, *Anchor*, *Lock*. You can find many *Navigations*, especially, from Wootten Wawen on the Stratford Canal to Gnosall on the Shropshire Union, and from Kilby on the Leicester to Gathurst on the Leeds & Liverpool.

There are *Boats* from Hayton on the Chesterfield to Loughborough on the Leicester, from Penkridge on the Staffs & Worcs to the widely-known thatched one opposite the Waterways Museum. There are pubs called the *Bridge* from Tibberton on the Worcester & Birmingham to others in the middle of Stoke-on-Trent and the middle of the Birmingham Canals.

There's also a *Longboat* in Birmingham, a *Grand Junction Arms* in Harlesden, and *Narrow Boats* both in the East End of London and at Weedon in Northamptonshire. And you can seek many other watery names, too, such as *Aqueduct*, *Pilot*, *Fisherman*, *Swan*, *Old Barge*, *Fish and Eels*, *Canal Tavern*, and even the *Rock of Gibraltar*, the *Cape of Good Hope* and the *Ship Aground*.

(*above*) Waterside pub at Boxmoor

(*below*) Pub with appropriate name on the Leeds & Liverpool

(*above*) Near Leighton Buzzard on the Grand Union Canal

(*below*) The *Cross Keys* near Penkridge on the Staffs & Worcs Canal

Waterway pubs also have other names which are nothing to do with water. There's a *Dog in a Doublet* on the river Nene, and many *Red Lions* and *White Lions* all over the country. There's a *Plum Pudding* and a *Cheshire Cheese* alongside canals, and an *Ash Tree*, a *Globe*, and a *Blue Lias*.

Animals, Fish, Birds and Flowers

If you are walking or boating along a canal you will see many growing things and quite a few moving creatures. It is certainly worth carrying identification books for the flowers, trees, animals, birds and freshwater fishes.

Plants seem to be much bigger and healthier alongside water, no doubt because they are never short of moisture. There are huge docks and tall pink-flowered willow-herb, as well as the shorter wild forget-me-nots. Yellow irises grow in the water's edge in June, and great balsam ('policeman's helmet' because of the shape of its flowers) may be up to six feet high.

Floating on the water may be yellow or white water-lilies. These more often grow in rivers, but they may, surprisingly, be found on the way to Slough. Look for the yellow marsh marigolds (kingcup), and for various reeds and rushes such as the reedmace, with its knobbly brown flower. This plant is often incorrectly called a bulrush. Along the Shropshire Union you may find large primroses in spring, and even smell wild garlic in one place. The Monmouthshire & Brecon Canal is especially prolific with spring flowers.

Under the water there are invariably weeds which

Birds, animals and flowers of the canals

boaters dislike as they get entangled with the propellers. Some weeds have large cabbage-like leaves and tough stalks, while others look more like long strings, or balls of green cotton-wool. Another plant has arrow-shaped leaves which bob under water as a boat approaches.

Besides the ordinary birds of the hedges and trees, there are several which especially live near water. Moorhens (water hens) swim about, and build their nests even on floating clumps of reed. Their chicks are like small fluffy balls, and soon swim. Ducks and drakes fly up in front of you, and swans sometimes peck at boats, either to defend their nests or to beg for scraps.

You may find coots with white beaks, and tall herons standing by the water ready to pounce on a fish. Perhaps the rarest sight is that of a kingfisher, which flies like a bright blue flash up the canal in front of a boat, landing on a bush and then flashing away as the boat approaches again. In the evening watch the swallows in summer darting down for insects. And at any time of day you can see wagtails wagging their tails on the towpath, or magpies holding a meeting in a field.

Animals are rarer than birds, and the only ones you are likely to see are water-voles, often wrongly called water-rats. These swim across the canal and dive when a boat approaches. Their homes are tunnels in the bank with underwater entrances. You may sometimes see animals in the fields around, especially rabbits and hares, and perhaps even a fox. But you'll be lucky to see a badger, for these interesting creatures are usually out only after dark.

It is difficult to observe fish, also, for the water in most canals and many rivers isn't very clear. But you may find an ugly pike lurking under the bank on the Leicester Grand Union, or small shoals of tiny fish scuttling near the edges anywhere. Fish seem smaller in canals, but all over the country anglers catch roach, dace, bream, perch and chub. There are certainly many fish under the water, even if you can't easily detect them.

Other living and growing things are common. There are beetles, spiders and snails, and in summer both midges and wasps will find you. Notice the dragonflies with their bright colours. Look at the towpath hedges, and at the willow trees along waterways, often with their weeping branches hanging right down to the water.

The canal network today. (*The numbers refer to the list starting on p. 158.*)

11 THE CANAL AND RIVER NETWORK TODAY

This section lists the inland waterways normally used by boats nowadays, but first a word about their very existence. It is only too easy to look at canals and take them for granted. In fact many of those still existing would have become derelict years ago but for the founding of the Inland Waterways Association in 1946, by Robert Aickman and others. Its members – all volunteers – have fought against apathy and even official opposition to retain and restore canals. They wish to see them fully used both for commerce and leisure. Over the years the IWA has given rise also to a large number of local societies and trusts, usually connected with a particular waterway, who also work and campaign to retain or revive their canal or river for use by all.

The full story of the IWA and the many smaller bodies will one day make fascinating reading. Enthusiasts, young and old, have rebuilt locks and dug out channels, raised large sums of money to pay for much of this, fought in Parliament and campaigned in public. Many historic fights have been won and restorations of such waterways as the Stratford Canal, the Warwickshire Avon, the Stourbridge, Erewash, Ashton and Peak Forest Canals and others, form landmarks in recent waterway history just as important as the early digging of the canals.

The value of the IWA and the local organizations

cannot be too highly praised and the fight continues. There is still apathy and still opposition to the use of waterways in Britain, much to the amazement and amusement of other countries. Thus membership of these voluntary bodies increases. The list of waterways in this chapter would be considerably shorter without this great restoration movement. And it will be added to yet.

The list shows all navigable waterways in common 'inland' use, as distinct from estuaries. As you have read, most are used mainly by pleasure boats, though many – if enlarged – could be of great value for carrying goods.

It has, as explained earlier, been impossible to omit rivers, since so many are integral to the waterway system. Usually, however, the lengths included are the 'locked' lengths, where the tide cannot penetrate. But a few tidal lengths are included where they are in common use by inland boats. For example, some tidal stretches of the river Trent, the river Thames, the Yorkshire Ouse and a short part of the Great Ouse are used by inland boats to move from one inland waterway to another. In these cases both the tidal part and the tidal lock are included in the list. Locks are broad unless otherwise stated.

The waterways in England can be identified on the map on page 156 by means of the bold figure numbers on the following list. An asterisk means that the canal or river is still not fully restored.

1 *Lancaster Canal, with Glasson Branch. 45½ miles, 6 locks*
All the locks are on the branch to the unusual Glasson Dock, with a sea-lock out to the estuary. The main

canal has no locks since the building of the M6 cut off
its northern end to Kendal. Isolated from the main
waterway system, the canal has a good channel with
plenty of boats, passes several large villages, and skirts
Lancaster on a massive aqueduct over the Lune.

2 Leeds & Liverpool Canal, with Leigh Branch and Rufford Branch. 142 miles, 104 locks

Solid as the rock of the Pennines, which must have
been used in building its locks and bridges. There is
a good channel on the whole, but the many towns –
especially in Lancashire – do produce rubbish. The
contrast between vandal-strewn Liverpool and the
moor-surrounded Pennine stretches is remarkable.
On the whole, though, this canal manages to pass its
towns in both Lancashire and Yorkshire quite
unobtrusively, with plenty of greenery even there.

There are over 50 hand-operated swing-bridges,
and the broad locks are sometimes difficult to work.
The Rufford Branch leads to a sea-lock out to the
river Douglas, and the Leigh Branch links with the
Bridgewater Canal, over moon-like territory south
of Wigan. There is a great embankment at Burnley
and many staircase locks in Yorkshire. There are also
the strenuous Wigan locks (23 of them), and a tunnel
at Foulridge once swum by a cow (1640 yd, 1500 m).

The locks of the Leeds & Liverpool, though broad,
are too short for full-length narrow boats on the
stretch between Leeds and Wigan. A special key is
needed to unfasten padlocks on some locks, and a
special large windlass is often useful. There are four
further locks on a short branch down to the docks at
Liverpool.

3 *River (Yorkshire) Ouse (as far as the Trent), with river Ure, river Foss, and Ripon Canal. 70½ miles, 6 locks*

These form a continuous waterway apart from the short river Foss coming in at York. The lower part is not for the nervous, or for flimsy boats, for there are tides and currents almost to York, and sea-going traffic and barges. Above Naburn Lock there are many boats to York, and delightful moorings in the city centre. The route is quieter northwards, becoming the river Ure without warning, with the Ripon Canal – only just over a mile long – containing the northernmost English lock still in use. Ripon is a further mile on foot.

4 *River Derwent. 38 miles, 6 locks*★

This is a beautiful waterway in process of restoration, with many more miles still to go up to Malton. There is a curious new lock in the barrage at the entrance from the Ouse, and of course tidal knowledge is necessary to reach the river by water.

4A *Pocklington Canal. 9½ miles, 9 locks*★

A 'tributary' of the river Derwent, this remote canal is also in process of restoration, though the furthest lengths are in doubt. It is a fine rural area, with nature reserves around.

5 *Aire & Calder Navigation, with Wakefield Section. 41½ miles, 17 locks*

Wide and deep, this is a commercial waterway, with varied traffic. There are many rural stretches, but no striking views. The interest lies in the barges, the trains of 'Tom Puddings' filled with coal, and the shorter but larger containers being pushed in threes to the power stations. The locks are large and electrified, worked by keepers from little cabins. The terminus, from Leeds and Wakefield, is at Goole – a busy port.

6 *Calder & Hebble Navigation. 2 1½ miles, 27 locks (plus 8 flood locks)*

A tough canal with character, needing unusual handspikes to operate some of the paddle-gear. It is hard work for the boater clambering through this industrial region up to the Pennines, but most towns lie back a little. Brighouse embraces the canal and there is striking scenery towards the upper end. At Sowerby Bridge the Rochdale Canal leaves – a trans-Pennine canal being rapidly restored. The basin there is worth visiting, with old warehouses coming back into use.

7 *Huddersfield Broad Canal (or Sir John Ramsden's). 3½ miles, 9 locks*

A short and sharp canal from the Calder & Hebble up to Huddersfield, with a remarkable lift-bridge near its end. It now continues for a short way into the Huddersfield Narrow Canal over the Pennines, which has the longest tunnel in the country. This has a lively restoration society.

8 *Sheffield & South Yorkshire Navigation. 43 miles, 28 locks*

A commercial waterway with an exciting future. After many years of compaigning it has been extensively modernized, offering a vigorous route from the West Riding via the Humber and to Europe. It is industrial and well-locked at its upper end (especially the not-to-be-missed 11 locks up to

Sheffield and its basin), but easier and more rural lower down. Officially it runs to the Trent at Keadby, but the main commercial traffic uses the New Junction (*q.v.*) to join the Aire & Calder to Goole.

8A *New Junction Canal. 5½ miles, 1 lock*
As mentioned above, this links the Sheffield & S. Yorkshire with the Aire & Calder. It was built as recently as 1905, as straight as an arrow, and with several opening bridges. Until recently they were opened manually by bridge-keepers with capstans, but they have now been electrified and made into push-button bridges.

9 *Manchester Ship Canal. 36 miles, 5 locks*
Not, of course, for pleasure cruising, but pleasure boats will be accepted under strict conditions. The traffic on this canal consists of quite large vessels and the whole canal is the 'Port of Manchester'. Built as recently as 1894, it is our most remarkable waterway, until recently taking ships into the heart of the city.

10 *River Weaver. 20 miles, 5 locks*
This river takes small ships but also has much pleasure boating. It can be reached down the intriguing Anderton Lift (see p. 88) and runs from a lake-like 'Flash' at Winsford down to extensive chemical works alongside Weston Point Docks, where there is a lock to the Manchester Ship Canal. Much salt is produced near the upper reaches.

11 *Bridgewater Canal. 40 miles, 1 lock*
This is the historic canal as eventually developed, except that the locks at Runcorn down to the Mersey

no longer exist. The single lock is on a short branch to the river Irwell at the head of the Manchester Ship Canal. The original canal from Worsley is now a branch linking with the Leigh Branch of the Leeds & Liverpool. The main line runs to Runcorn, with a short connection at Preston Brook with the Trent & Mersey.

12 *Ashton Canal. 6½ miles, 18 locks (all narrow)*
A canal with a recent interesting history. It was derelict after 1961, and many wished to fill it in. But vigorous efforts by enthusiasts, including some huge clearance operations, resulted in full restoration by 1974. It is now part of the popular 'Cheshire Ring'. From the Peak Forest Canal at Dukinfield it runs through its many locks down to the heart of Manchester, where it joins the private Rochdale Canal.

12A *Rochdale Canal. 1½ miles, 9 locks★*
Originally 33 miles with 92 locks across the Pennines from Manchester to Sowerby Bridge, this is being rapidly restored, with various lengths in use. A vital section of 9 locks in Manchester links the Ashton Canal and the Bridgewater Canal in the Cheshire Ring. A special fee has to be paid by boats, as this canal is still privately owned.

13 *Peak Forest Canal. 15 miles, 16 locks (all narrow)*
This canal is in two natural parts: the upper length from Marple to Whaley Bridge and Bugsworth, which was never derelict; and the lower part to the Ashton Canal, which was closed and then restored along with the Ashton (q.v.). The upper part has some spectacular valley views. The lower part has the

delightful flight of 16 locks at Marple, the striking Marple Aqueduct, and then some more industrial urban lengths to Dukinfield.

14 *Macclesfield Canal. 27½ miles, 13 locks (all narrow)*
The southern 1½ miles is strictly Trent & Mersey, but nowadays the 'Macc' is taken as starting at Hardings Wood Junction on the Trent & Mersey, from where it later crosses the T & M on a 'canal flyover' as it goes north. It is often high enough on the hillsides to give views over the Cheshire Plain to Manchester Airport. Eastwards it looks up to the moors, with Mow Cop and The Cloud hanging over it. The locks are grouped near Bosley, and have – unusually for narrow locks – pairs of gates at each end. This canal has massive stone bridges, curving in near the water, and some attractive turnover bridges for the towpath.

15 *River Trent (as far as the Humber/Yorkshire Ouse). 95 miles, 13 locks*
Apart from a canal link through Nottingham, this is wide and deep, with big locks. The navigable part starts near Shardlow, and below Nottingham there are lock-keepers, with most locks electrified and some barge traffic. The heavy manual locks, out of working hours, have to be operated by boaters, and all seem as deep as a canyon. There are scattered pubs, and Newark is a good calling place. Five miles lower down the tidal part begins and pleasure boats need special care and advice. But this is a necessary link with the Fossdyke to Lincoln and Boston, the Chesterfield Canal to Worksop, and the Sheffield & S. Yorkshire to Yorkshire and across the Pennines.

16 *River Ancholme. 19 miles, 1 lock*

This is an isolated river, not really accessible to inland waterway boats, since they must tackle the Humber to get there. It is mostly straight, running through flat country, with Brigg as its only centre of population.

17 *Chesterfield Canal. 26 miles, 16 locks (9 of them narrow)*

This now runs only from the Trent to Worksop; the rest is largely out of use, including especially a long tunnel at Norwood. The first 7 locks are broad, though not suitable for 14 ft boats. From Retford the locks are narrow, as the canal passes through the Dukeries to Worksop. This is a pleasant rural canal, and though boats must use the Trent to reach it, the effort is worthwhile.

18 *Fossdyke Canal and river Witham. 48 miles, 3 locks*

Treated as one waterway, this comprises the ancient (Roman) canal from the Trent to Lincoln, and then the river Witham to Boston and eventually the Wash. It is a flat journey with wide views, particularly of Lincoln Cathedral. Often lonely, it comes to Boston under the view of the Stump there. At Lincoln it has the unusual experience of passing between Woolworths and Marks and Spencers.

19 *Llangollen (or Welsh) Canal. 46 miles, 21 locks (all narrow)*

Strictly a branch of the Shropshire Union, and supposed to be closed in 1944, this is one of our busiest pleasure canals. It is also unusual in feeding water down from the Dee to reservoirs at its lower end. Pleasantly rural, it leads finally just into the

Welsh mountains and Llangollen. It has some Dutch-like lift-bridges, and tunnels and aqueducts, including the spectacular Pontcysyllte, 307 m (1007 ft) long. ★The Montgomery Canal is a branch through Welshpool, 35 miles and 26 locks, which is under active restoration despite problems with lowered bridges.

20 *Shropshire Union Canal with Middlewich Branch (20A). 76½ miles, 50 locks (33 of them narrow)*
A fine canal with variety, winding and with broad locks near Chester, bold and straight south of Nantwich, with high embankments and deep cuttings. Cows, sheep, horses, and even goats and pigs are on view in places. It takes boats from the Black Country to the Manchester Ship Canal. Busy in parts, but down past Chester's walls on to the Wirral it is less so. There is a fine canal boat museum at the terminus at Ellesmere Port.

21 *Trent & Mersey Canal. 93½ miles, 76 locks (69 of them narrow)*
This is probably the canal that 'has everything' – plenty of locks, tunnels of character, industry, farming, pubs, woods, flowers. There are broad locks at the Trent end, but later on they are narrow, and some are precariously quaint. Stoke-on-Trent, and especially Harecastle Tunnel, leave quite an impression, and the many locks of 'Heartbreak Hill' beyond are not easy to forget. The views down to the Weaver from the northern end are breath-taking, while there are three not-too-straight tunnels along the way. This, of course, was the canal much associated with James Brindley, though he died before it was finished. It no

longer joins the Mersey, but certainly justifies its original name, the Grand Trunk.

21A *Caldon Canal. 20 miles, 17 locks (all narrow)*
Strictly a branch of the Trent & Mersey, this is another canal restored from near-dereliction. It runs from Stoke up to the hills, then down the Churnet valley. There are fine views once industry is left behind, and even a little commercial use from unusual boats carrying pottery. The main line runs to Froghall Basin through a low tunnel, and there is a branch going almost to Leck, past a wide pool and another short tunnel.

22 *Erewash Canal. 11½ miles, 15 locks*
Short and industrial but fascinating. Runs from the Trent up to the old junction with the Cromford and Nottingham Canals at Langley Mill, where the basin has been restored. There are several pubs and some memorable railway sidings. The northern end is quieter.

23 *Staffordshire and Worcestershire Canal. 46 miles, 45 locks (all narrow)*
A grand route from the Trent & Mersey to the Severn, this was an important part of the original Grand Cross of canals. Although the locks are narrow, there are two broad locks available out of the basins at Stourport to the Severn. Mostly rural, the 'Staffs & Worcs' does creep quietly past Wolverhampton. Its locks are usually well spread out, with an intriguing trio at the Bratch. There are hills, trees and sandstone in the south, and the basins at Stourport are a delightful area of canal history.

24 *Birmingham Canal Navigations. 90 miles, 95 locks (all narrow)*

The above figures exclude the Birmingham & Fazeley Canal, which is usually thought of in its own right now. The BCN is impossible to describe briefly, but this fascinating network is not as industrial as it sounds. Despite some grim patches there is considerable greenery and much peace. The canals meander throughout the Black Country, with two long tunnels between north and south. There are several branches worth following, including one to a remote basin below Chasewater Reservoir. There are lock-flights around the outskirts, power-stations and rubbish, motorways on stilts and yellow gorse. No canal addict can miss this region.

25 *Stourbridge Canal. 5½ miles, 20 locks (all narrow)*

Short and steep, from a truly rural beginning at the Staffs & Worcs Canal to a quick climb into the Black Country. The views back during this climb are spectacular, though even more so after the first locks in the BCN. There is a branch to Stourbridge, newly dredged, and the 16-lock flight was once the scene of a historic restoration battle.

26 *Birmingham & Fazeley Canal. 15 miles, 38 locks (all narrow)*

Strictly part of the BCN, and the 24 locks from Salford ('Spaghetti') Junction certainly are. But outside this area it gradually becomes rural, with blackberry bushes and a lone pub called the *Dog and Doublet*. An unusual swing bridge leads to the last stretch before joining the Coventry Canal at Fazeley.

27 *Ashby Canal. 22 miles, no locks*

This is a fascinating cul-de-sac rural canal in a mainly non-rural area. It never went to Ashby (de-la-Zouch), but ended at Moira, and the final miles to Moira have been lost. The terminus now is just beyond short Snarestone tunnel. The sides are shallow, and there are weeds, with yellow irises in June. Some pleasant villages lie near by, with a boatyard at Stoke Golding. It is an attractive canal, especially to boaters who dislike locks.

28 *Grand Union Canal, Leicester Line, with Market Harborough and Welford Branches. 73 miles, 60 locks (18 of them narrow)*

This leaves the main Grand Union line at Norton Junction and runs up to the Trent. There is a magnificent 21-mile summit level between the narrow locks at Watford (Northants) and Foxton. There is a staircase of four locks among the Watford ones, and the ten locks at Foxton are in two staircases of five each, drawing crowds of spectators. Northwards from this point, after the interesting branch to Market Harborough, the locks are broad and often old. At Leicester the river Soar begins, and this can flood at times. The locks are spread out and, after Loughborough, the towers of Redhill power station signal the junction with the Trent.

29 *Worcester & Birmingham Canal. 30 miles, 58 locks (all narrow except the last two to the Severn)*

This is a striking canal, running level out of Birmingham for 14 miles, then dropping rapidly to the Severn in the next 16 miles. The level length includes Birmingham University and a 2493 m

(2726yd) tunnel which has been extensively repaired. There are four other tunnels on the canal. 42 of the locks occur in 5 miles and, as a result, there are wide views from the top of this slope. Locks are a little more spread out during the final length to pleasant Diglis Basin, at Worcester, near the cathedral and the porcelain works.

30 *Stratford-upon-Avon Canal. 25½ miles, 55 locks (1 broad, rest narrow)*

An interesting canal. The southern part was derelict, but has been restored by volunteers. The northern part is shallow in places, leaving the Birmingham area on the level and then dropping fairly quickly to Kingswood Junction, where there is a link with the Grand Union before the National Trust section begins. This has 36 locks in 13 miles, some unusual barrel-roofed lock-houses, and beautiful scenery. There are several aqueducts, including a striking iron trough on brick pillars at Edstone. The terminus comes, after a backdoor entry to Stratford, in the basin in front of the Memorial Theatre. The broad lock leads out to the Avon.

31 *Coventry Canal. 38 miles, 13 locks (all narrow)*

Though busy with through traffic to the north, the short length from Hawkesbury Junction to Coventry is worth the detour, ending in a basin above the city. There are some dull stretches northwards, but after Nuneaton, and especially after the 11 locks at Atherstone, the country opens up. Then industry returns at Tamworth, to be followed by country again for eleven level miles to the Trent & Mersey. These last eleven miles were built for the original company by other companies, and the difference in bridges, etc., is noticeable.

32 *River Nene. 65½ miles, 37 locks*
Very different from the canals, but linked to the Grand Union by the 17-lock Northampton Branch, and leading to the canal-like Middle Level Drains. The locks are spectacular, most of them having great steel guillotine gates at the bottom end, to be raised by many turns of a large handle (156 at some locks), with as many turns to lower them. The river is mostly wide and deep, with views across water-meadows to villages on the foothills, and sheep and cows grazing on the banks. Many swans and Canada geese, and unusual isolation, since the towns as well as the villages stand back from the river which has parks alongside. There are fine if costly moorings at Peterborough, near the cathedral, and at Oundle a marina where the river surrounds the town in a horseshoe.

33 *Middle Level Navigations, with Old Bedford River.*
92 miles, 7 locks (not 'broad', but wider than the
normal 'narrow')
Strictly 'drains', for that is their purpose, but boats have used them always. This is a strange and lonely network, mostly below sea-level, and consequently has high banks. Hardly any habitation alongside except for the town of March, and the Dutch-like villages of Upwell and Outwell on the way to the Great Ouse. The waters are wide and deep, with weeds in summer, and a profusion of anglers. They form a boating route between the Nene and the Ouse, but have their own remote attraction.

34 *Monmouthshire & Brecon Canal. 33 miles, 6 locks (rather wider than 'narrow')*

A picturesque isolated canal, running on the hillsides above the Usk valley. It has been renamed, but is mostly the original Brecon and Abergavenny Canal, though it is well above the latter town. The canal is overlooked by mountains. It is often lined by trees and spring flowers are abundant in their season. There are several villages near by, and some simple old lifting bridges, as well as an electric one. A fine stone aqueduct carries the canal over the Usk below Brecon.

35 *River Severn. 42 miles, 5 locks*

Wide and deep, with large locks, and a tendency to flood rapidly in rain. Two canals and a river join it; it leads to the Gloucester & Sharpness Ship Canal to avoid the dangers of its lower estuary. There are high banks, and mooring is not easy in towns, but Worcester bestrides it. There are a few bankside inns. The locks are electric, worked from little cabins by keepers.

36 *Gloucester & Sharpness Ship Canal. 17 miles, 1 lock*

Takes quite large ships, avoiding the treacherous Severn estuary, up to Gloucester Docks. There are 16 movable bridges, all but one swinging, with bridge-keepers in fascinating houses. Sharpness is a busy port, but pleasure boats can moor in the old arm by the river. At the other end, mooring in Gloucester Docks is like another world.

37 *River Avon (Warwickshire). 46½ miles, 17 locks*

This has a fine history of restoration, with the length to Evesham being reopened in 1965, and the rest to

Stratford – a more difficult task, needing new locks – in 1974. It is deep and winding, with orchards and rolling country, though sometimes a chilly welcome to boats. Where it is possible to moor, Pershore and Evesham are pleasant, and the moorings at Stratford attract as many sightseers as the Theatre opposite.

38 *Grand Union Main Line, with branches in London, and to Slough, Aylesbury and Northampton. 176½ miles, 215 locks (45 of them narrow)*

This is our longest canal now, though it consists of a number of different original companies, especially when its Leicester Line is considered. In London there are two ways to the Thames – via Brentford, or on the Paddington Branch, through the heart of London via the Regents Canal to the East End and Limehouse Basin. Going north, the canal climbs up to the Chilterns, then drops slowly through the countryside to the new city of Milton Keynes and to the historic canal-village of Braunston. In Warwickshire there are locks with interesting paddle gear; 46 of them are in the vicinity of Leamington. Then industry appears as the canal nears Birmingham; a rather grubby narrow-locked terminus links with the Birmingham & Fazeley at Salford Junction. The Aylesbury Branch has 16 narrow locks, and the Nene link to Northampton has 17.

39 *Oxford Canal. 77 miles, 44 locks (all narrow)*

A very popular canal, shallow and sometimes short of water. There are long meanders and much remote country in the southern part. The northern length has been straightened, and is perhaps less interesting. Banbury has neglected its canal, and Oxford, too, does little about it. But the parts between are delightful, with several small villages.

40 *The river Great Ouse, with Little Ouse, Lark, Wissey, Cam, New Bedford River, and lodes. 147½ miles, 23 locks*

Quite a cruising network in itself, but not easily accessible from the main system of waterways. Rather like the Thames in places, though the lower lengths have high banks. The locks usually have guillotine gates, though there are new ones at the Bedford end (recently reopened) of more standard pattern. There are interesting towns such as St Ives, St Neots and Bedford itself higher up, and Ely lower down. Cambridge is up the Cam. The lower tributaries (Lark, Little Ouse and Wissey) are much quieter and more remote.

41 *Norfolk and Suffolk Broads and Rivers. Approx 115 miles, no locks*

Highly organized cruising area, often crowded, but the original mass leisure waterways. No locks, but finding moorings is strenuous. Wide and deep channels in most places, but some low bridges. The actual 'broads' are wide lakes, but most of the cruising is on rivers, one going up to Norwich. Several villages are geared to the boats, and have ample provisions. Good views from Ranworth church tower.

42 *River Thames (to Grand Union Canal at Brentford). 129 miles, 45 locks*

Nearly as easy to cruise as the Broads, and all the locks are worked by keepers. But there are many boats, some luxury types. There are luxury pubs, too, and expensive moorings at superior towns. Above Oxford the river is quieter and less sophisticated.

43 *Kennet & Avon Canal. 86½ miles, 104 locks*★
This is the most staggering example of voluntary restoration, since the project is so vast. For example, at Devizes there are 29 locks in 2 miles to be restored. But a vigorous Trust is pressing on, and full restoration is almost complete. The canal is really two river navigations linked by pure canal, forming a route from the Thames at Reading to the tidal (but dangerous) Severn. There are several pleasant towns such as Newbury, Hungerford, Devizes and Bradford-on-Avon, and of course the waterway flows through the heart of Bath. There are some fine stone aqueducts, interesting old pumps restored at Claverton and Crofton, and trip-boats available on all the opened stretches. The full restoration is a task worth supporting.

43A *River Avon (Bristol). 4½ miles, 1 lock*
This is the non-tidal extension of the Kennet & Avon, forming a link between Bath and Bristol. Inland boats do not normally venture on the tidal length to Avonmouth and the Severn without sea-going skill and a pilot.

44 *River Lee (or Lea). 28 miles, 19 locks*
This runs from London docks to the middle of Herts. The lower end is commercial and not attractive, though there are large reservoirs hiding alongside. Lock-gear is unusual, and every lock has its house. Above Enfield the scenery is pleasanter, and there are many leisure activities alongside, with occasional pubs

as well. Many boats pass through Stanstead Abbots; Ware has a fine rose-surrounded lock. The terminus at Hertford is rather dreary.

45 *River Stort. 14 miles, 15 locks*
A tributary of the Lee, this is more canal-like, and indeed its locks are not really 'broad'. It passes Harlow, but almost unobtrusively, and runs pleasantly by Sawbridgeworth to a surprising terminus by a car park in Bishop's Stortford, with supermarkets a trolley-walk away.

46 *Basingstoke Canal. 31 miles, 29 locks★*
Now owned by two county councils, and with a lively Society busy on restoration, which is almost complete. Remarkable work has been done already on lock-walls and gates, and it will form a useful extension of the river Wey cruise for the large population of the south east. All the locks are in the first half, and the final 15 miles, through Aldershot and Fleet, are level; the present terminus is at the collapsed Greywell Tunnel. The length to Basingstoke has been abandoned.

47 *River Wey and Godalming Navigation. 19½ miles, 16 locks*
The southernmost limit of the waterway network, this leaves the Thames near Weybridge and crosses pleasant countryside, although it is so near to habitation. This waterway comes under the National Trust, and passes near the Royal Horticultural Society Gardens at Wisley. Several handy inns. Mooring in the heart of Guildford is attractive, and the final length to Godalming is especially delightful.

Canals in Scotland

Caledonian Canal. *60 miles, 29 locks*

Very different from any English canal, this is really a
number of lochs linked by canal sections, and passes
through fine scenery. The lochs can be quite rough,
while the canal locks are large, passing boats up to
150 ft (46 m) long and 35 ft (11 m) wide. At Banavie
the greatest staircase of locks in Britain, 8 of them,
lifts boats up or down. There are many unusual sights
along the waterway, from a hand-wound rail bridge
to the 700 ft deep Loch Ness, maybe with its monster.

Crinan Canal. *9 miles, 15 locks*

A short canal, avoiding a 132-mile passage round the
Mull of Kintyre for fishing boats and yachts. Again
there is fine scenery and some cuts are through solid
rock, with views down over flatter country. Crinan
itself is a delightful village with its canal basin and
lighthouse.

Other canals

The *Exeter Canal* is still used, but is more of a short
sea-boat waterway, 5 miles long with two locks.

There are also other canals in various states, and
usually at some stage of restoration, ranging from the
highly likely to the rather optimistic. Parts of the
majority of these may be in use by boats, though
often by unpowered ones only. Such canals include
the following: Stroudwater, Thames & Severn,
Bridgwater & Taunton, Grand Western, Wey &
Arun, Droitwich, Cromford, Driffield, Huddersfield, Grantham, Montgomery, Wendover, Forth &
Clyde, Union, Rochdale – further lengths, Chesterfield – further lengths.

GLOSSARY

Here are some of the words used specially on inland waterways, or used in special ways there. Many of them have been explained in greater detail elsewhere in this book. Curiously – although they have been used along waterways for many years – some are not normally found in their waterway meanings in dictionaries.

aqueduct A bridge for carrying a waterway over a road, railway, valley, etc. (*See* Chapter 5.)

balance beam The wooden, metal (or even concrete-filled) arm sticking out over land from most lock-gates. You push against this to close or open the gate.

barge Usually applied to boats of about 14 ft (4.27 m) or more in width, on inland waters.

basin A wider place at the side or end of a waterway, where boats can moor to be loaded or unloaded.

bollard A post of wood, metal or concrete for tying up a boat with ropes.

bridge hole The width of a waterway under a bridge.

butty Usually a narrow boat without an engine, being towed by one with an engine.

clough (say 'clow') A name often used for paddles in the north. Even pronounced 'clew' at times.

compartment boats Special engineless boats which can be pulled or pushed in trains.

cut The name often used for a canal, because it was

cut from the ground in the first place ('the cut').

dredger A machine – usually a form of boat, or carried in a boat – which scoops mud and rubbish from waterways.

fender An item made of rope, plastic, rubber or wood, which is hung alongside a boat to protect its sides from damage.

gongoozler Someone who stands idly about – especially at locks – just gazing at what is happening.

guillotine gate A kind of lock-gate which slides upwards instead of swinging sideways.

hire boats The pleasure boats offered by many firms for holiday cruising.

hotel boats Pleasure boats with small cabins, lounge, dining room, etc., on which people can stay for a week or more as in a hotel. Often they are narrow boats cruising in pairs.

junction A place where one waterway joins another.

keb A sort of long-handled rake, used for dragging rubbish from waterways, especially at locks.

legging The way boats were taken through tunnels before they had engines, if there was no towpath. Men lay out sideways and 'walked' along the tunnel side or top.

moor (or **moor up**) To tie up a boat safely at the waterside.

motor Besides meaning an engine, this word is also used for an actual **boat** which has an engine, especially if it is a narrow boat towing a butty (engineless).

narrow boat (*See* Chapter 8).

paddle The general name given to the covers over the openings at locks which allow water in and out. (*See* Chapter 6.)

paddle-gear   The variety of machinery for opening and closing the paddles. (*See* Chapter 6.)

pound   The stretch of water between locks.

puddle   The specially-mixed clay which lines the beds of canals.

ram's head   The rudder-post of a traditional narrow boat, often topped by a special rope-knot which is called a **Turk's head**.

reservoir   The very necessary source, often specially dug, to supply water to a canal, since water is continually used up by locks.

roving bridge (or **turnover bridge**)   A bridge where the towpath crosses from one side of the canal to the other. Often curved in a special way so that the towrope doesn't have to be unfastened when the horse crosses over.

shaft   The name usually given to the long pole carried on boats, often used for pushing them off the mud if aground.

short boat   A boat as wide as a barge, but only about 60 ft (18.29 m) long instead of the more usual 70 ft (21.34 m), built for use in the shorter locks of most of the Leeds & Liverpool Canal.

side-pond   A small pond at the side of some locks, made to save water. Some of the lock water is run into this pond instead of down the canal. It can then be run back in to help fill the lock for the next boat in the other direction.

sill (or **cill**)   The solid ledge, usually of concrete, or concrete and wood, against which the bottom edges of lock-gates close.

staircases   Locks which are so close together that there are no pounds of the canal in between. The locks thus lead into each other. (*See* Chapter 7.)

steerer The old name for the person steering a canal boat.

stoppage The name given to the closure of a waterway for a time to do repairs.

stop-planks Lengths of wood that can be slid down **stop grooves** at narrow places such as bridges or locks. They then make a dam so that water can be pumped out to do repairs. Or they may be inserted quickly to stop a leak from draining the canal.

summit level The highest level of a canal. This is the length into which the water from a reservoir must be fed.

tiller The arm, fixed to the rudder-post, which the steerer uses to steer a boat.

towpath (or **towing-path**) The path built alongside canals and some rivers for the towing-horses to walk along.

weir An overflow arrangement, usually alongside locks, for water in one pound to run down into the next if the upper pound is too full. Some weirs are in the open, some run underground. On rivers, a weir is in the form of a dam. (*See* Chapter 3.)

winding hole (pronounced as the wind that blows) A wide place on a canal where long boats can be turned round ('winded').

windlass The bent handle used for turning the paddle-gear of most locks. All boats on canals need to carry windlasses.

USEFUL BOOKS

Books on canals are not easily found in bookshops, and may have to be ordered. An excellent postal service (postage extra) is provided by the *Inland Waterways Association (Sales) Ltd, 114 Regents Park Road, London NW1 8UQ*. They supply most current publications, including historical and pictorial books, guides, maps and children's books. A stamped addressed envelope will bring the latest list.

Many good waterway books are out of print, but *M. & M. Baldwin, 24 High St, Cleobury Mortimer, Kidderminster, Worcs DY14 8BY*, and *Shepperton Swan, The Clock House, Upper Halliford, Shepperton, TW17 8RU*, have many second-hand ones.

Books listed below are all fairly recent, but may not all be in print. If out of print, libraries or the firms above may have them.

Historical Books

For the serious student, Charles Hadfield's books are essential. A whole series of regional volumes appear under the title *The Canals of the British Isles*, with a 'parent' book, *British Canals*, updated regularly. All are published by David & Charles.

Robert Wilson publishes inexpensive booklets, with many old photographs dealing with past life on canals. There are also numerous small books on individual canals, published from various sources, obtainable from the IWA.

Here is a selection of other general historical books:

Hanson, H., *Canal People*, David & Charles

Ransom, P. J. G., *The Archaeology of Canals*, World's Work

Rolt, L. T. C., *Narrow Boat*, Eyre Methuen

Russell, R., *Lost Canals and Waterways of Britain*, David & Charles

Weaver, C. R. and Weaver, C. P., *Steam on Canals*, David & Charles

Woolfitt, S, *Idle Women*, M. & M. Baldwin

Burton, A., *The Canal Builders*, Eyre Methuen

Blagrove, D., *Bread upon the Waters*, Pearson

General Books

Owen, D., *Exploring England by Canal*, David & Charles

Baldwin, M. M. and Burton, A., (ed.), *Canals – a New Look*, David & Charles

Smith, P., *Discovering Canals in Britain*, Shire

Smith, P., *Discovering Craft of Inland Waterways*, Shire

Edwards, L. A., *Inland Waterways of Great Britain* (the statistical 'bible'), Imray Laurie

McKnight, H., *The Shell Book of Inland Waterways*, David & Charles

Lewerey, A. J., *Narrow Boat Painting*, David & Charles

Burton, A., *Backdoor Britain*, Deutsch

Hutchings, C., *The Story of Our Canals* (for children), Ladybird

Russell, R. (ed.), *Walking Canals*, David & Charles

Warner, P., *Lock-keeper's Daughter*, Shepperton Swan

An inexpensive series of small books by John Gagg looks pictorially at canals now: *Locks, Tunnels, Narrow Canals, Broad Canals, Waterway Landmarks, Canals in a Nutshell.* Belmont Press, 29 Tenby Avenue, Harrow HA3 8RU.

GENERAL INFORMATION

Maps and Guides
Stanford's Inland Cruising Map shows all canals, with locks, tunnels, distances, etc., in relation to roads and towns.

Douglas Smith's maps give much detail of various waterway areas, showing everything of note along the routes. The IWA Sales list includes all those available.

There are many small guides to individual canals, obtainable from the IWA. For the canal network generally, the *Nicholson/Ordnance Survey Guides to the Waterways* are in three parts, *South*, *Central* and *North*. There is an excellent *London's Waterway Guide* (Cove-Smith, C.) published by Imray Laurie.

The Inland Waterways Guide is published each year by Brittain Publications and the IWA. It gives brief details of waterways with small sketch maps, and lists boat-hire firms.

Films and Slides
The British Waterways Board has films and slides available. (*See Address* below.)

Museums
There are several museums on the canal network. *The Waterways Museum* is the original British Waterways one, at *Stoke Bruerne, Nr Towcester, Northants NN12 7SE*, near locks and a tunnel. Phone Northampton

862229. However a bigger one is now open in Gloucester docks, phone Gloucester 25524.

The *Boat Museum*, a magnificent site at Ellesmere Port has numerous historic canal boats afloat and much instructive material under cover.

The Black Country Museum at Dudley has much working canal material among its other exhibits. It is also near the vast Dudley Tunnel. *Tipton Road, Dudley, W. Midlands DY1 4SQ.*

The Canal Exhibition Centre at Llangollen gives a recorded commentary on canal history, by the canal. Phone Llangollen 860702.

Hiring Cruisers

Firms offering cruisers for holiday hire along canals are given in *The Inland Waterways Guide* (see above – Maps and Guides). There are also agencies, such as Hoseasons, Blakes and Boat Enquiries, which act for groups of firms.

Boat Trips

Short boat trips are available at many places, some of the boats even being drawn by horses. You may find local advertisements, and *The Inland Waterways Guide* also lists firms offering such trips.

Magazines

There are two monthly magazines concerned with inland waterways and usually obtainable from newsagents. They are *Waterways World* (address: *Kottingham House, Dale St, Burton-on-Trent, DE14 3TD*), and *Canal & Riverboat* (address: *9 West St, Epsom, Surrey KT18 7RL*). *Motor Boat & Yachting* also contains material on inland waterways each month.

Waterways News, the magazine of the British Waterways Board, is also available to the public. (See address below.) The Inland Waterways Association publishes national and regional magazines for its members. (See address below.)

The British Waterways Board

This is the official body responsible for most of our waterways, dealing with every aspect of its canals and rivers for both commerce and pleasure. It issues licences, and has a very helpful Information Centre. This not only answers enquiries, but has useful material available, including films and slides. Details from the *Information Centre, British Waterways Board, Melbury House, Melbury Terrace, London, NW1 6JX.*

Boat-users on the Board's waterways can obtain information about any unexpected repairs or closures by ringing the 'Canalphone' service. For northern areas: (01) 723-8486. For southern areas: (01) 723-8487.

The Inland Waterways Association

Anyone really interested in canals should consider joining the *Inland Waterways Association, 114 Regents Park Road, London, NW1 8UQ*, without whose volunteer labours since 1946 many canals in present use would be derelict. It has Branches covering the whole of England and Wales, and varied local meetings and activities are organized. The Association is the most comprehensive source of published waterway material, and will also help enquirers in many ways, eg, by providing information for schools.

There are separate but similar associations in Scotland and Ireland, and readers living there should make enquiries as to the addresses of present secretaries.

Canal Societies and Trusts

In addition to IWA Branches covering the whole country, there are over 50 local societies and trusts, most of them also members of the IWA. Each naturally has a special concern for its particular waterway. Secretaries tend to change, but enquiries along a canal, or from the IWA, will unearth the current one.

INDEX

Bold numbers denote main references; italic numbers denote illustrations.